Competitive Intelligence Rescue

Competitive Intelligence Rescue

Carolyn M. Vella and John J. McGonagle

 PRAEGER™

An Imprint of ABC-CLIO, LLC

Santa Barbara, California • Denver, Colorado

Library of Congress Cataloging-in-Publication Data

Names: Vella, Carolyn M., author. | McGonagle, John J., author.
Title: Competitive intelligence rescue : getting it right / Carolyn M. Vella and John J. McGonagle.
Description: Santa Barbara : Praeger, [2017] | Includes bibliographical references and index.
Identifiers: LCCN 2017012602 (print) | LCCN 2017024160 (ebook) | ISBN 9781440851612 (ebook) | ISBN 9781440851605 (hardcopy : alk. paper)
Subjects: LCSH: Business intelligence.
Classification: LCC HD38.7 (ebook) | LCC HD38.7 .V44 2017 (print) | DDC 658.4/72—dc23
LC record available at https://lccn.loc.gov/2017012602

ISBN: 978–1–4408–5160–5
EISBN: 978–1–4408–5161–2

21 20 19 18 17   1 2 3 4 5

This book is also available as an eBook.

Praeger
An Imprint of ABC-CLIO, LLC

ABC-CLIO, LLC
130 Cremona Drive, P.O. Box 1911
Santa Barbara, California 93116-1911
www.abc-clio.com

This book is printed on acid-free paper ∞

Manufactured in the United States of America

Contents

Preface

It is surprising at how many people who work in businesses, both large and small, some for many years, know very little about the industry and the sector in which they work, their competitors, and sometimes even about their own company.

You know that even though you have been working with the same people for many years, you may not even really know much, if anything, about the people with whom you work. If you do not know these things and if you do not know the environment in which you work, how is your product or service supposed to be the best in your industry? How are you and your firm supposed to succeed?

The first thing you must do is learn about your business environment. That means looking at the arena in which you function. You must look at your customers. Where are they? Where do they live and where do they purchase and consume your product? These will vary, of course, depending upon the industry. A bar is different from a bakery, which is different from a stock broker, so both the questions and answers will be different.

Then you must understand those with whom you are competing for this business. First, who are your competitors? Second, how are they competing? Third, what will they probably be doing next?

To learn all these things, you use a process called "competitive intelligence." This business management process can be conducted by professionals, individuals trained to do it. Or you can do it yourself if you learn how to use the research and analysis techniques in the proper way. But there is more to it than the mechanics of finding and then analyzing data.

Essentially competitive intelligence, or CI as it is called, is a method of analyzing your business, your business environment, where you are now, where your competitors are now, where they are going, and where they want to be in the future. Sometimes, you are just interested in one aspect of your business, perhaps one product that is losing market share to a competitor.

Maybe this has not happened before. It is new and you have to know why it is happening, so you can recover.

Of course, CI includes more than just analyzing some data. It requires management and communication—two areas all too often overlooked when anyone discusses CI, whether in their firm or in their own work.

CI is not something brand new. It is an established discipline, which allows you to develop actionable intelligence for businesses and even for nonprofits. That intelligence lets you know what your competitors are doing, what they are capable of doing, and what they will or may do. In fact, it is also useful to do the same kind of research and analysis on your suppliers, partners, distributors, and even key customers. Knowing what they are really doing, what they can do, and what they are likely to do next lets you do better in the marketplace. But the best CI is that which is actionable. By actionable, we mean intelligence that you use to make decisions and to take some action—that is something well beyond something that is "nice to know."

CI has matured and expanded since it started in the 1980s, but, unfortunately, those practicing it today are too often doing it badly. Let us be a little more specific. Over the past 25 years, CI has changed in a variety of ways.

For example, CI has been widely and profitably adopted by some business sectors, such as the pharmaceutical industry. But other sectors of the business community have not adopted it or, having adopted it, have not used it effectively.

Some have even downgraded it to the point of ignoring it. That is due in part to the small number of properly trained professionals available to do CI correctly.

Even where CI has been adopted, a lot of CI programs were the victims of budget cutbacks starting with the 2008 recession. In some firms and industries, the CI teams still have not recovered from that. But it is also due to the chronic failure of businesses to come to grips with how CI really works and how it can help.

That is where we come in. In addition, CI is getting, well, old. CI still tends to rely on principles first developed in the 1980s—and earlier—and very often looks back to its historic roots in government intelligence, that is, spying, for additional guidance.

That last fact is really odd because, during the same period, government intelligence has undergone significant changes, particularly since 9/11. In fact, many people involved in training those in government intelligence now look to the private sector for help in dealing with certain kinds of intelligence, what is often called open-source intelligence. Open-source intelligence? That is the kind of thing CI lives for. It means dealing with data that are openly available and accessible by legal and ethical means.

Not all these changes have been bad. For example, increasingly some basic level CI is being done by executives, managers, and staff who have no or only limited formal training in CI, but who need and produce CI for their own use. We call these the Do-It-Yourselfers or DIYers.

A problem arises however when they are expected to provide CI for themselves without any assistance or training, or are supposed to provide CI for others to use as well. That work product is often, predictably, poor. And that, in turn, contributes to a decline in executive and managerial interest in CI, and ultimately in their support for CI.

But the way we collect, use, and manage CI can make it very powerful. We just have to get past these problems. CI can still be a particularly valuable and powerful tool, supporting everything from strategic planning to marketing and new business development to human resources.

That is the purpose of this book—"Getting It Right." By walking you through cases based on our years of experience in CI, this book will enable anyone using, or seeking to use, CI in business, in the nonprofit arena, or in education, to evaluate what he/she is doing and what others are doing. And then, using this book as a guide, you can determine what is being done wrong, what is not being done that needs to be done now, and how to fix it.

To start with, we are going to walk you through different cases, based on real situations, that present some of the most common problems in managing, developing, or using CI. Of course, the names we use are not the real names of our clients.

Then, we are going to present you with simple, proven methodologies detailing how to spot problems, how to educate others to bring about improvements and changes, what changes to make, and how to test and show that the changes are working. We are going to do that by taking you along as we deal with these cases, letting you know what we see and how you can look for it. And, at the end, we will look back on what we have shown you to help you extract even more value from this.

Whom can we help? Well, first, we can help any manager, executive, or owner now getting and using, or trying to use, CI. These people are typically in medium-sized and large enterprises including businesses, law firms, hospitals, nonprofits, and universities. Because there are so many types of organizations that can and should use CI, we will just call them all "firms."

Also, this book is aimed at anyone, inside or outside of a firm, who is now providing CI to themselves or to managers and executives, whether or not they carry CI in their title or job description.

In addition, we want to help the manager, executive, or owner who has no access to CI right now. These people typically run small and medium-sized businesses and some nonprofit enterprises.

Finally, we want to help the newest members of the CI community, the DIYers—the largest and fastest growing part of the CI community.

After you read this book, you will be able to diagnose what problems with CI you face, and will have the tools to make it and manage it better, and to show that the changes are vital and effective. This is not a text book—it is a how-to-do-it-better-now book. That is why we are talking to you this way.

Once you improve your CI operations, or add CI where it is necessary, you will see immediate improvements in your firm's performance, in its planning, in its competitiveness, and in its agility.

As you can see, we have written this as if we are talking with our clients, to each other, and to you. That puts us all in the middle of the process of rescuing your CI program. We have tried to make this the way that we see it. For example, unless there is a very unusual situation, we interview our client's officers, managers, and employees in these assignments one-on-one or two-on-one. And we do not discuss what these interviewees have said with others. That way, officers are not influencing their direct reports, and peers are not going to trim what they say depending on what others are saying or have already said. We always take notes during the interviews, so what we lay out here is always based on them. This book reflects that.

From time to time, we have inserted working materials into the narrative. The memos are ones we would have written for this kind of assignment. Any "news reports" are created from facts in the public record, but are not taken from any specific publication. The emails are typical of the discussions we have with clients and with each other. That all means you will feel like you are standing next to us while we work to help our clients—and ultimately to help you.

To keep things manageable, each case study will deal with only one or two key issues of the many we worked with the client on solving, even though the issues we worked on may have been, and often are, much more numerous and complex. That means you may have to review a couple of cases to deal with your situation. To help you navigate more precisely, throughout we break up the text with headings and label the memos and other materials so that you can drill down to find what you need.

Carolyn M. Vella and John J. McGonagle

1

The Language of Competitive Intelligence and of This Book

THIS BOOK

In this book, while the cases are based on very real situations, we never use the real names of our clients or of their executives and employees. To protect our clients and to keep it simple, we have massaged and restated the facts and elements of our relationships and the clients' problems, and then related conversations and emails that are composites. Usually the details are much more complex than we show to you.

When we created a firm name, to avoid using a real one, we have checked to make sure that we did not find a firm with that same name in the industry we are talking about. Of course, someone could adopt that name after this book is finished, but that would be a coincidence.

Since our clients communicate with us in a variety of ways, as we do with them, we have included examples of those varieties of communications. So, you will listen in on conversations, read email exchanges, and review memos, and draft corporate documents, checklists, and even slides for presentations.

COMPETITIVE INTELLIGENCE

Before we start digging into the cases of different firms to help rescue them from their competitive intelligence, CI, problems, let us review what we know about CI. Although we could get very technical here, we will not. We just want to remind everyone that CI is the process of collecting data, on a legal and ethical basis, and then transforming it into actionable intelligence.

By actionable, we mean something you can use, that you will use, as opposed to something that is just "nice to know." A quick way to understand this is to ask yourself or the person you are working with if there is some decision that cannot be made or an action that cannot be taken without CI. That CI is actionable. Otherwise it is not actionable.

From here on, we are going to look at several different companies, big and small, public and private. We will dig into each of them, seeking to understand what they are doing, what they say they need to do, what they really need to do, how to do that, and how to see that they have accomplished meaningful change. For you, it will be like working beside us.

We will try to avoid jargon. If we need to introduce a term, whether from CI or elsewhere, we will define it the first time we use it and give you the traditional acronym, if there is one. However, we will avoid as much industry-specific jargon, catch phrases, and slang as we can for two reasons: one, such language is often unintelligible to those outside the specific industry, and two, they often fall out of favor. Both of these factors indicate that this sort of language becomes unhelpful and even confusing as time passes.

2

Diagnostic Quizzes and Questions

In the next chapter, our first case study focuses on collecting CI, particularly in the do-it-yourself (DIY) context. The balance of the book deals with case studies that combine the collection and analysis of CI with organizational issues, as well as with creating a program protecting a company against the CI efforts of competitors. The reason for this combination is that organization is vital to providing and distributing actionable CI. You can have people who can collect raw data effectively or people who can analyze that data to produce intelligence, but, if there is a disconnect between the consumers of that intelligence, in CI often called the end users, and the collectors and analysts, then all that CI is worthless.

We have developed a series of quizzes that form the core of our approach a CI rescue. But, before asking these questions and taking these quizzes, do what we do—find out the facts and take great care to separate them from opinion, yours and theirs.

What do we mean by that? When approaching a CI rescue, your own or someone else's, you have to probe for the truth. Let us show you how to do that.

FIRST-LEVEL DIAGNOSTIC QUESTIONS

Here, we start by identifying the organization, or a part of it, which needs the help, and then drilling down to develop more basic information on it. Here are the ways we usually start this. You can start this way, too.

- What does your firm do? Describe your firm in three or four sentences. Then, research the firm, and see how it is described in directories, credit reports, industry sources, legal filings, and the like. You may be surprised to see there is often a difference between your description and these descriptions. Ask yourself why?

- Who are your major competitors? After answering, cross-check this, too. Just because you "know" firms A, B, C, D, and E are your major competitors does not mean that you are correct. Always cross-check that. Why? Let us give you an example. We worked with a client that wanted to know how key competitors in four market segments were planning for acquisitions and mergers. The client provided us with a list of the top five firms in each of the four segments, taken from interviews with its own senior executives. When we cross-checked, we found that each of the client's four lists had identified three of the top five competitors correctly. But, on each list, two of the five competitors initially listed were no longer a major force in that segment or even still in that line of business at all. And worst of all, in every one of the four segments, there was at least one company no one at the client had identified, but which was now among the top five. Talk about wearing blindfolds! What is worse is that this kind of blind spot is not at all uncommon. Except for those directly involved in the sales process dealing with customers, the competitive views of many managers and executives can be months or even years out of date.

- How do you check on how valid your view of your competitors is? Ask your customers who they think are their major customers—and why. As above, check public sources too. We conducted training for a client's technology managers where one exercise for those attending was to list their top five competitors. We then produced lists from several sources, all listing different "competitors" of the client. We asked those attending to explain the differences.

- What is the internal market for your CI? That should include both those who are, in theory, receiving CI reports, materials, and briefings and those who probably should be receiving them but are not doing so now. Also, try and identify the DIYers, or at least the areas within the firm where there are DIYers. As you will see in several of the case studies, sometimes the existence of DIYers will be uncovered only during your CI rescue operations.

- What CI is being delivered to the internal clients? When and how is it being used? You probably need to first find out if it is being used at all. Being used means it assists in making decisions and taking actions. Then, find out who produced it. That is not always the same as who provided it to the internal clients. You may find out, as we did in one case, that the CI team uses outside contractors to supplement its work or to provide specific products, but that many of its end users were not aware of that.

- Speaking of outside contractors, if there are outside CI contractors, who are they and what intelligence products do they provide? How long have they been doing that? Are their products being used? By whom? How useful are they? Here, you will often find that the longer they have been working for your firm, the more likely it is that you need to review and update their mission to meet your needs and those of your internal client(s).

That ends the first-level questions, setting up the context for you and our rescue. You will see how we handled them in the first part of each case study.

From here, you must dig deeper into the people, the processes, and the linkages to find out what needs repairing, what needs upgrading, what needs to be added, and what needs to be scrapped during your CI rescue.

DIAGNOSTIC QUIZZES

To dig deeper, you (and we) should apply the following deeper dive diagnostic questions—they represent the kind of questions you should be asking about what you and your firm are doing to get CI, to manage that process, and to use that CI effectively. In these diagnostic questions, when we talk about your CI team, we are referring to each resource your firm uses to develop and communicate intelligence—your internal CI specialists, a single person, your in-house DIYers, non-CI staff, and/or your outside CI firms—whether they work together or not.

To make this process less threatening to our clients, we usually call them "quizzes," not questions. These quizzes provide a detailed way to dive into the elements that extensive research and experience have shown are what the "best of the best" CI programs and individuals really do, and do well and consistently. They are not and cannot be complete. Also, since they reflect real-world experiences, they necessarily overlap, as even the best CI practices are not identical.

There are a lot of statements under each question, so that the quiz can identify small differences, such as the presence or lack of training on primary data collection versus on secondary data collection. Just remember that they are a guide.

For example, we did not include any question or statements on defending against the CI efforts of your own competitors. That is not because it is not important. In fact, it is. Rather such programs are not nearly as widespread as they should be, and where they are in place, they may be run by a CI manager, by corporate security, or even as a part of a broader, cybersecurity program. We have covered this topic later in the book, where it arose in the context of a company with no CI program at all.

When you use these quizzes, you should respond to each of these statements below the overarching question with a response like "yes, we do that," "maybe we do, we probably do that, or we do it only occasionally," or "no, we do not do that." When you cannot answer "yes," it is time to figure out how to change things so that the answer will be yes. Where you answer "maybe" or "no," review our case studies for help in executing your own CI rescue. You have probably found something that needs work. And do not hesitate to dive deeper for more details. The more that you know what is actually going on—as distinguished from what people think is going on—the better you can develop and manage your own CI rescue.

Some questions and their statements are designed to dig into the situation from the CI team's perspective; others dig in from management's perceptions. Always carefully compare management's answers with the CI team's answers. Any difference, even seemingly minor, can be a warning of emerging, but still invisible, problems or management issues. Solve them now or suffer from them later.

We used these in each of our cases, indicating which *key* elements of the quiz our client met ("yes") following our initial evaluation of the CI rescue, and where the client fell short ("maybe/perhaps" and "no") so you can share our quick overview of what we were told and saw before we started work on executing that CI rescue.

How is our CI team staffed, trained, and managed?

Here, we are trying to get the heart of the rescue—to the people who provide the CI, whether they use it—DIYers—or provide it to others. Who are they, what skills do they have, and where are they lacking in the tools that they need? This digs into their perspective and perceptions.

- Our CI team, individually or collectively, has specific **training** on CI.
- Our CI team has a process to train interested and appropriate personnel in the skills and tools necessary to collect **secondary information**.
- Our CI team has a process to train interested and appropriate personnel in the skills and tools necessary to collect **primary information**.
- Our CI team has a process to train interested and appropriate personnel in the skills and tools necessary to analyze and then **disseminate information** to appropriate end users.
- Our CI team has a process to train interested and appropriate personnel in the skills and tools necessary to **manage individuals** performing CI data collection, analysis, and dissemination.
- Our CI team or individual, individually or collectively, has **experience** in developing and providing CI.
- Our CI team or individual, individually or collectively, has current **industry knowledge**.
- Our CI team or individual, individually or collectively, has good written and oral **communication** skills.
- Those responsible for our CI activities clearly understand CI's objectives, target audience, and expected measures of **success**.
- Our CI team or individual, individually and collectively, has a clear understanding of who their **internal end users/customers** are.
- In its **skills training**, our CI team has developed its own methods to help the team or individual members increase their industry and/or technical knowledge to be able to assess key industry factors, their knowledge of our firm's products and services, and their personal skills, including oral and

written communications, relationship and network building, and creative thinking.

- Our CI team, individually and collectively, has a clear understanding of the **needs** of its internal end users/customers.
- All members of our CI team understand the **CI processes** in which they participate.
- The training provided for members of our CI team dealing with collecting primary information includes **techniques** such as selecting the appropriate people to contact, conducting both telephone and face-to-face interviewing, developing and making effective use of internal and external networks, developing and making effective use of external networks, and working trade shows and industry meetings.

How does our CI team get its direction on targets, on its data collection, and on deliverables?

This question focuses on management. Note that we here are looking both at targeting and at how the critical directions on data collection are provided and who provides them.

- Our CI program meets its **users' needs** on an ongoing basis, determined by a defined process and predetermined objectives.
- The CI team produces intelligence reports and assessments on our competitors and/or emerging **threats** it believes are most important.
- Our CI team has clearly understood objectives and consciously identified the **target audience** it aims to serve, such as the sales force or our top executives.
- Our CI team has a systematic process for identifying and defining its **intelligence needs**.
- Our CI team focuses its intelligence efforts on competitors and products/technologies that **management** has identified as important.
- Our CI team has specific criteria to decide what **types of data** are to be collected and which competitors it will be collected on.
- Our CI team interviews management regularly to understand their **intelligence requirements** and uses those requirements to focus our CI efforts and allocate resources.
- Our CI team uses both **primary and secondary** intelligence sources.
- Our CI activities have a set of clearly defined **objectives**, with clearly identified end users.
- Business/program/product/technology managers are responsible for providing some of **their own CI**.

Where does our CI team get its data?

Here, we are digging into the CI research process. This overlaps with the previous question because directing research and doing it overlap. That is because providing actionable CI involves continual feedback among all of the parties.

- Our CI team uses **secondary sources** of information (public materials, analysts' reports, etc.) to learn about key competitors and/or new products and technology.
- Our CI team uses **primary/human sources** of intelligence in addition to secondary sources.
- Our CI team uses our management's **intelligence requirements** to guide collection.
- Our CI team has developed and uses both internal and external **networks** to assist in its data gathering.
- Our **employees** all report information about our competitors or relevant emerging threats and opportunities to the appropriate managers.
- Our CI team has established a set of legal and ethical **guidelines** covering the gathering, use, and communication of CI. These guidelines are clear, specific to our firm's industry, and directly apply to the information-gathering situations all our employees might face.

What intelligence does our CI team provide?

Here, the focus is on deliverables: what intelligence is provided, to whom, when, and in what forms. There is no one right way to do this—for every audience, and sometimes for every member of that audience, there are good ways to do this, and bad ways too. The CI providers must learn what works. They also must continually review who should be getting the intelligence and in what form, as that will constantly change.

- Our CI team prepares **profiles** of our competitors, including their business plans and strategies.
- Our CI team delivers **timely** assessments and briefings on our competitors' plans and actions, as well as new product/technology developments, to managers who have the authority and responsibility to act on that intelligence.
- Our intelligence program systematically collects, analyzes, and disseminates intelligence to those people in our firm responsible for business planning and **decision making**.
- Our CI team **analyzes** our competitors' business plans and strategies to predict and anticipate their future actions.
- Our CI team produces assessments that address several possible outcomes of competitor actions and that identify the **threats and opportunities** those outcomes present for our company, its business plans, new products, and the like.
- Our CI team distributes its **CI findings** throughout the company to those who need them or makes them available online to those who need them.
- Our CI team provides significant **trend analyses** to determine potential new forces in the firm's business environment that other parts of the firm, focused on performing their daily functions, might not be aware of.

- Our CI team sees its mission as including not only as being providers of CI to specific end users/customers but also as being **ambassadors of CI** within the entire firm, using training as a communication vehicle.

What does our firm do to help our CI process?

Adequate and appropriate management support for the CI process is critical to a successful program. And, support is much more than merely providing an adequate budget. Categorizing these statements can often highlight where specific support is needed, but is currently lacking.

- Our management is making **visible efforts** both to support and to use CI.
- Our firm recognizes CI as a **legitimate** and necessary activity in today's marketplace.
- Our firm's management is **actively involved** in CI activities and ensures that the CI team or individual is adequately funded.
- Our CI team ensures those employees involved in CI activities are given **basic intelligence training**.
- Our company has a formal set of legal and ethical **guidelines** designed specifically for CI.
- Our employees are aware of our CI activities and how to **contribute** to and/or benefit from that activity as determined by our CI team.
- Our firm's **legal department** regularly reviews our organized CI activities, as well as any DIY CI activities, to ensure that they are being conducted legally and ethically.
- Employees, at all levels in the firm, understand and support the importance of the firm's **commitment** to CI.
- Our firm provides **education** on ethics and legalities of CI to all employees involved in any intelligence activities, even to DIYers and others outside of the CI team or individual.
- Our management's use of CI is measured in their regular **performance reviews**.
- Our firm ensures that our CI team members are provided **professional education** in the areas they are primarily responsible, such as data collection and analysis.
- In addition to professional CI training, our firm provides **advanced training** for the CI team, including training on managing our CI operation.
- Our CI process is regularly evaluated by all the participants to **continuously improve** lines of communication.
- Our firm's management at all levels fully supports **participation** in internal CI networks and makes it a part of the participant's job description.
- Our firm's management ensures that those who should be using CI or contributing to the provision of CI have their **work reviews** include an evaluation of these efforts.

What do our managers and executives expect from and get from the CI team?

Here, we have the reciprocal of the view from the CI team—what does management see, what does it get, what does it expect, and how does it see the CI team performing? Also, remember to highlight anywhere that answers here vary from answers to the previous question by the CI team.

- Company management—at all levels—**supports** our intelligence activities and uses CI effectively in business planning and decision making.
- Our firm **budgets** both time and money to the CI process.
- The CI team has **ongoing relationships** with the firm's key decision makers, even those who are not direct end users/customers.
- Our business managers require CI inputs for key **program reviews**.
- There is regular **two-way communication** between the CI team and our senior management.
- Business/product/program/technology managers all expect CI to have a tangible and measurable **impact** on company decisions and business performance.
- Our CI program is run by a small group of people, professionally trained to produce CI for the management unit's **varying needs**, including business planning and decision-making.
- Our CI end users/customers consider our CI activity to be **effective**, to regularly meet its intended objectives, and to be serving their predetermined and communicated needs.
- The ethical and legal guidelines governing our CI program are distributed throughout our firm and are included in training that our employees and our **outside contractors** attend.
- Our CI program meets its predetermined objectives and its **results** are measured in terms of their impact on the firm's business performance.
- Our management is **willing to hear** things that they might not want to hear from the CI team or individual.

What results has the CI process achieved at the firm?

For CI to survive in any firm, it must produce. However, in many firms, there is no effective, formal process for evaluating the successes—and failures—of CI on a continual, objective, and formal basis. Where CI produces results, it is because the intelligence is accurate, professionally provided, and meets management's needs. But, for management's needs to be met, management must communicate its needs clearly and on and ongoing basis to the CI team. It must also commit to use the CI in decision making. Actionable intelligence requires that management act on it.

- Our firm can identify the past and current **impacts** of the CI process, such as changes in management processes or in our strategies.
- Our CI team can demonstrate that its intelligence has been **acted on**, that is, that CI contributes to decisions or actions leading to beneficial outcomes.
- CI directly affects decision making at the **senior level** in our firm.
- Our CI team's work, in collaboration with management, has changed the way our management understands itself and the entire firm in relation to the external environment and has **directly impacted** their strategic planning and business objectives.
- Our CI activities meet end user/customer needs on an ongoing basis; objectives for that performance show steady **advancement.**
- Our CI team can demonstrate how our legal and ethical guidelines are effective in controlling illegal or unethical intelligence data gathering and are encouraging **safe, yet effective**, use of CI.
- Our CI team can demonstrate that there are demonstrable **links** between our CI training, our CI activity, and our business results, based on actions taken or avoided because of our CI.
- Our CI team as identified measures by which it determines if its activity is **effective**. These might be changes in market share, competitive "win rates," timely employee and executive awareness of competitor strategies, other competitor activities, or new product/service features, or impacts on related business objectives, such as customer satisfaction or financial performance.
- Our management uses CI at all levels of **decision making** (i.e., strategic, tactical, budget, planning).

3

DIY CI

About the Company

We have been contacted by an investment group, Casual Investors, that is looking to make a new investment. Now, the company is looking at a restaurant that meets its needs, even though it has told us that it knows that restaurants have a lower rate of success than other businesses. The company made this selection from among four potential investments after some consideration. They all meet the profile that the investment group says it likes.

Its Management, Owners, and Employees

Casual Investors is made up of six people who have invested together in various ventures over the years very successfully. Recently, it added a new junior partner. In this case, Casual Investors is looking to back an experienced restaurant manager and kitchen staff. It is not looking to open its own restaurant, but to buy an existing one that needs its financial backing to make it more successful and more profitable.

A Look at Its Competitive Environment and Market Profile

Casual Investors found a restaurant whose owner is looking to sell. The owner is retiring due to his age. This restaurant has been a very popular place for about 15 years or so. It is on the corner of Main Street and a major street that crosses Main. Of course, there are other restaurants in the general area, including other potential investments the partners briefly looked at, but rejected. They are all right in the heart of a medium-sized city, near the performing arts center. This target restaurant is within walking distance of the performing arts center. So, there is, or so the partners think there is, a nice base of potential customers coming into town every weekend, and during most of the spring and summer on weekdays, beyond the usual local walk-in crowd.

There is a bar at the target restaurant, but the restaurant currently focuses on meals service, not on the bar. It is serving lunch and dinner regularly, with brunch, but not breakfast, on holidays. This seems to be the usual practice in this city.

The restaurant will need the investors' money to update the restaurant, change the decor, update the kitchen, perhaps hire another chef, and possibly hire more or even new staff. In any case, the current owners are ok with making a complete change. From the partners' comments to us, we assume that they will change the entire style of food. Right now, the style is American food with a touch of whatever happens to be popular at that moment.

What were its plans? What is coming next?

Casual Investors plans to be investing a total of $1 million in the restaurant. The company wants to have 10 percent of its investment capital recovered yearly, starting at the end of the first year after the first day of the opening of the revamped restaurant. The investment contract has not yet been signed, but the partners seem determined to go forward with it.

Status of Intelligence Operations

Casual Investors has no intelligence operations and conducted no CI on nearby restaurant competitors.

What problems/issues were identified by the client?

John: What do they want? Are they looking for market research?

Carolyn: Actually, no. They want to understand what the competing restaurants in the neighborhood are doing and what their strengths and weaknesses are. Also, they want to know if any of them currently have expansion, contraction, or renovation plans. The idea is to understand how the competition is operating now, and, if possible, how they will operate in the near future, as well. Also, they want to know what the competitors see as the busy times and days, what are the troughs, that sort of thing. They are looking outward so they can do better than the current owner does.

In addition, the partners seem to have perception problems. They told us that restaurants have a very high failure rate, around 90 percent for the first year. But, according to a recent Ohio State study, the 90 percent failure rate is a myth. The failure rate, in the first year, the worst year, for non-chain restaurants, is about 25 percent, they said. It makes me wonder what else the partners may be missing.

OUR PERSPECTIVES

What were the real problems there? Why are they different from what the company said they were?

Doing Its Own CI

Carolyn: There is a woman involved with Casual Investors, Jane, who says she knows a little about CI and has even read a couple of our books. She is new to the firm, so she does not have the kind of money to put into the project that some of the others have her work in lieu of cash, if it is all right with us.

I don't have a problem using her to work with us if you don't. We would have to hire someone to help us anyway. We'll have to teach her a bit about DIY CI and direct her, but if she already has an interest, she might be excellent.

We would design the project, but she would work with us, and learn as she works. We are the paid mentors, she earns a share of the investment, and Casual Investors develops its own CI capabilities. That's not a bad arrangement. She might be an excellent aide. After all, if non-locals like us start going in to the same restaurant time and time again over a short time, we become "known and valued" regular customers and we don't want that. That is too high a level of visibility. We need other people to do CI on the place with us, so Jane would do it.

We have to train her how to find out certain things, what she has to see, how to really read a menu as well as to see where the competitors are saving money for themselves, such as with the quality of the utensils and plating, also on the decor. It should be an interesting project. I don't think people realize how intricate this can be. She has to learn to see the competition's operations and plans through their customers' eyes as well as through their owners' eyes. For example, there is a restaurant supply store not far from here. It's a big one with a wide variety when it comes to quality of utensils and plating. This appears to serve all of the competitors, so it has to be checked into so she, or we, can evaluate how much the competition is spending on their customers.

We'll have to know exactly how they see their business. What is their vision? What is their plan? Are they fine dining or they a trendy "now kale must be somewhere on the plate" establishment? Where will they be going—if anywhere?

John: I can see where you are going on this. It sounds like a simple project, but it isn't. You have Casual Investors' partners who want CI before they invest their money and that is understandable. In fact, it is very smart. You have the restaurant staff that will be helped by the CI that's being done for Casual Investors as new owners, not to mention that the current owners need, or at least want, the new investment. The CI will make the difference as to whether the new restaurant gets the investment, and if it does, how well it will succeed.

Carolyn: We also have to check the neighborhood, zoning, building structures, and so on. These are all the basic things that must be checked on before we go anywhere else. If there is any issue with the liquor license, for example, we can have a problem right at the start. By the way, how long does it take to get a liquor license there? If Casual Investors buys the restaurant, instead of just investing in it, can the restaurant transfer the one they have now or does the legal new entity have to reapply? How long will it take to get another license? Also, how long will it take to complete a redo of the interior itself, and that includes the kitchen? Are you going to talk to Jane?

John: OK. I will talk with her about how to do this once we get Casual Investors' go ahead.

Key CI Diagnostic Quiz Results

How is our CI team staffed, trained, and managed?

At this point, there is no team or individual providing any CI. However, there is one individual designated to provide CI in the future.

Yes

The designated CI individual has current industry knowledge.

The designated CI individual has good written and oral communication skills.

The designated CI individual has a clear understanding of who her internal end users/customers are.

The training for the designated CI individual will deal with collecting primary information using techniques such as selecting the appropriate people to contact and conducting both telephone and face-to-face interviews.

Maybe/Perhaps

The designated CI individual has an incomplete understanding of the needs of her internal end users/customers.

No

The designated CI individual does not yet have specific training on CI.

The designated CI individual has no experience in developing and providing CI.

The designated CI individual does not clearly understand CI's objectives, target audience, and expected measures of success.

The designated CI individual does not yet understand the CI processes in which she will participate.

How does the CI individual get its direction on targets, on its data collection, and on deliverables?

At this point, there is no team or individual providing any CI. However, there is one individual designated to provide CI in the future.

Yes

The designated CI individual has clearly understood objectives and consciously identified the target audience she aims to serve, her partners.

The designated CI individual will focus her intelligence efforts on products/technologies that her partners have identified as important.

No

There is no current CI program that meets its users' needs on an ongoing basis, determined by a defined process and predetermined objectives.

The designated CI individual does not yet produce intelligence reports and assessments on competitors and/or emerging threats she believes are most important.

The designated CI individual does not yet have a systematic process for identifying and defining the partnership's intelligence needs.

The designated CI individual does not yet use primary or secondary intelligence sources.

Where does our CI team get its data?

At this point, there is no team or individual providing any CI. However, there is one individual designated to provide CI in the future.

Yes

The designated individual will use secondary sources of information (public materials, analysts' reports, etc.) to learn about key competitors and/or new products and technology.

The designated CI individual will use primary/human sources of intelligence in addition to secondary sources.

The designated CI individual uses her management's intelligence requirements to guide collection.

No

The designated CI individual has no internal and external networks to assist in her data gathering.

The designated CI individual has not established a set of legal and ethical guidelines covering the gathering, use, and communication of CI.

What intelligence does the designated CI individual provide?

At this point, there is no team or individual providing any CI. However, there is one individual designated to provide CI in the future.

Yes

The designated CI individual will distribute her CI findings throughout the partnership.

No

The designated CI individual does not now prepare profiles of competitors or analyze competitors' business plans and strategies to predict and anticipate their future actions.

The designated CI individual does not now provide significant trend analyses to determine potential new forces in the firm's business environment.

What does the firm do to help the CI process?

At this point, there is no team or individual providing any CI. However, there is one individual designated to provide CI in the future.

Yes

The partnership is committed to making visible efforts both to support and to use CI.

The firm recognizes CI as a legitimate and necessary activity in today's marketplace.

The firm is ensuring that the designated CI individual is provided professional education in the areas she is primarily responsible, such as data collection and analysis.

The partnership's CI process will be evaluated by all the partners to continuously improve lines of communication.

No

The firm's management is not yet actively involved in CI activities and ensures that the CI individual is adequately funded.

The partnership does not have a formal set of legal and ethical guidelines designed specifically for CI.

What do the partners expect from and get from the CI individual?

At this point, there is no team or individual providing any CI. However, there is one individual designated to provide CI in the future.

Yes

The partnership supports intelligence activities and plans to use CI effectively in business planning and decision making.

The designated CI individual has ongoing relationships with the firm's partners.

Maybe/Perhaps

The partners appear willing to hear things that they might not want to hear from the designated CI individual.

What results has the CI process achieved at the firm?

At this point, there is no team or individual providing any CI upon which the partnership has acted. However, there is one individual designated to provide CI in the future.

Where and how did we solve the client's real problems and help the client?

Doing Their Own CI

> **Jane:** I am excited about this project. It is my opportunity to dig into the business and to learn about competitive intelligence at the same time. I think that will make the ultimate operations of the new restaurant even better and strengthen Casual Investors' ability to make future, better investments.

What is CI?

> **John:** Let's start with an understanding about what competitive intelligence, what we call CI, is, and what it is not, ok? Let's go over a couple of overhead slides that may help you.

What Is Competitive Intelligence (CI)?

- Two elements:
  - Use public sources to develop data (the raw facts) on the competition, competitors, and the overall market environment.
  - Transforming, by analysis, that data into information (usable results) able to support business decisions.
- In CI, public means all information you can legally and ethically identify, locate, and then access.

> **John:** Let me walk you through this. This focuses on the fact that competitive intelligence, which I will call CI from now on, involves both data collection and analysis. Data collection is not enough. Also, the way that you collect that data must always be legal and ethical. We are not "spies," engaged in espionage. That is illegal.
>
> **Jane:** That means you cannot take trade secrets, right?

John: Yes—if in fact they are trade secrets. Without getting too technical, for something to be a trade secret, the owner must take ongoing steps to keep it from becoming pubic. So just stamping it a trade secret and doing nothing else to protect it does not make it one. There has to be more.

Also, you might consider having the partnership draft a statement of ethics, just so that you are all "on the same page." It is easier to deal with a demanding client, and that is what your partners will be, who might push for unethical behavior if you do not have something in writing you both can rely on. Ok?

Jane: I will see that we do that. The partners are very strong on ethical behavior and this will resonate with them.

A Quick Look at Competitive Intelligence (CI) Terms:

- The CI process
- Data collection
- Analysis
- Creating and using CI
- Types of CI

John: Now why do you think that I will talk with you about definitions at this point?

Jane: The briefing, is it going to get very technical?

John: No, but that's a good guess. As you do more research and analysis, you will need to, and hopefully want to, learn more. So, you need to know how people in CI talk and write about what they do to continue to learn.

So, here is brief memo we prepared for you detailing some key terms you will want to know as you learn more. I thought just listing them in an overhead was a little much to digest, so you can review this when you need to.

KEY CI PROCESS TERMS

Decision maker: In CI, the individual or group for which an intelligence evaluation is prepared. Also, known as the end user or customer.

KITs/Key Intelligence Topics: Topics and issues that "keep management up at night." Pronounced "kits."

KIQs/Key Intelligence Questions: Questions for the CI function to answer, which are usually developed from KITs. Pronounced "kicks" or "quicks."

CI cycle: Process of establishing CI needs, collecting raw data, processing them into finished CI, and then distributing it to end users (who then use it). Also, includes feedback among the various steps in the cycle.

KEY CI DATA COLLECTION TERMS

Target: A specific competitor, or one or more of its facilities, business units, or other units on which your work focuses.

Data: Raw, unevaluated material. They may be numeric or textual. Data are the ultimate source of information, but only become usable only after they have been processed and analyzed.

Primary research: Research seeking original data. Usually refers to interviewing people or developing original data.

Secondary research: Research involving the summary, collation, and/or synthesis of existing research and data. Sometimes also called "desk research."

Pushback: A CI analyst talking to you about CI needs does not merely listen to what you say, write it down, and arrange to deliver it in three weeks. The analyst asks, and reasks, questions about what you want, why you want it, in what form you want it, when you want it, and what you will do with it when you get it.

Linkage: In CI, the connection between two or more different data sources, enabling a researcher to move from one to another.

Half-life: Every bit of intelligence data and analysis has a half-life, that is, period of time after which it loses half of its value. It may be one day, one week, one month, or even years.

Elicitation: Apparently ordinary conversation that is skillfully aimed at drawing out key data without alerting the interviewee that it is being done.

Closing the loop: Having individuals whom you or your CI specialist interview or try to interview referring you back either to secondary resources or to individuals whom you have previously tried to interview or interviewed. Can also apply in secondary research. This usually marks the end of your research work.

KEY CI ANALYSIS TERMS

Information: The material resulting from analyzing and evaluating raw data, reflecting both data and judgments. Information is an input to a finished CI evaluation—it is not the finished product.

Analysis: In general, an examination of facts and data to provide a basis for effective decisions. Analysis often involves the determination of cause-and-effect relationships. In CI, analysis involves evaluating and interpreting the facts and raw data to provide finished intelligence to support effective decision making.

Competitor analysis: Competitor analysis involves an assessment of strengths and weaknesses of current and potential competitors. It aims at bringing all relevant sources of competitive analysis into one framework to support effective strategy creation, strategy and tactical execution, and monitoring and adjustment.

False confirmation: When a piece of data appears to come from multiple independent sources, but in fact comes from only one source.

Mirror-imaging: Assuming that your target can or will do what you could or would do in its place.

Disinformation: Incomplete or inaccurate information from a target designed to mislead others about its intentions or abilities.

KEY TERMS FOR TYPES OF INTELLIGENCE

Competitive intelligence (CI): CI consists of two overall activities:

> First, use of public sources to develop data (raw facts) on competition, competitors, and the market environment.
> Second, transformation, by analysis, of that data into information (usable results).

Business intelligence: An old term for CI. Also, it is used in knowledge management (KM) to describe the product of KM activities.

Types of CI (Helicon's Own Typology)

Competitive technical intelligence/technology-oriented: Intelligence activities that allow a firm to respond to threats or identify and exploit opportunities resulting from technical and scientific changes.

Strategic intelligence/strategy-oriented: CI provided in support of strategic, as distinguished from tactical, decision making.

Competitor intelligence/target-oriented: Focuses on competitors and their capabilities, current activities, plans, and intentions.

Market intelligence/tactics-oriented: Focused on the very current activities in the marketplace. Look at it as the qualitative side of quantitative data research conducted in many retail markets.

KEY TERMS FOR CREATING AND USING CI

Intelligence: Knowledge achieved by a logical analysis and integration of available information data on competitors or the competitive environment.

Competitive scenario: An analysis of what one or more competitors can be expected to do in response to changes in market and other conditions affecting their activities. Based on a profile of each competitor, including estimations of its intentions and capabilities, and stemming from a study of its past actions and of the perceptions, style, and behavior of its present and future management. Each competitor's actions are studied against the same set of expected market conditions and changes.

Fundamental disconnect: When the creator of the CI and the end user are separate, the creator cannot require that the end user actually use the CI. This is not an issue in DIY CI!

SWOT/strength–weakness–opportunity–threat analysis: Strategic planning method used to assess the strengths, weaknesses, opportunities, and threats involved in a project. Involves specifying objective of project and then identifying both internal and external factors that support or impede obtaining that objective.

Gaming: An exercise that has people either acting as themselves or playing roles in an environment that can be real or simulated. Games can be repeated but cannot be replicated, as is the case with simulations and models. It is also known as war gaming or scenario playing.

Reverse engineering: Discovering technological principles of a device, object, or system through analysis of its structure, function, and operation.

Patent mapping: Visualization of the results of statistical analyses and text mining processes applied to patent filings.

> **John:** I know that this is a lot. Any questions about these?
>
> **Jane:** Yes—Are these meanings standard in the CI business or do people and firms have their own long, slang, that sort of thing?
>
> **John:** Good question. Most people use the same terms. There are a few differences in how the CI cycle is described. Also, not everyone uses KITs and KIQs, but everyone in CI knows, or should know, what they are and how they are used. We labeled where the terms are ones that we developed.

CI versus Market Research

CI versus Market Research (MR)

- *CI*
  - Largely qualitative
  - Driven by soft data
  - Involves future trends, projections
  - Focus on competition, competitive environment, capabilities, andplans
  - Largely external focus—us versus them

- *MR*
  - Largely quantitative
  - Driven by hard data
  - Involves present data
  - Focus on customers, pricing, products, and current actions
  - Largely internal focus—us versus them

John: Here I am trying to draw a broad distinction between market research and CI. Obviously, I am just looking at the clear majority of CI practitioners and how they work in general. You can always find a market researcher who looks at competitors' plans and a CI practitioner who is dealing with very quantitative issues. My goal is to help you see that there are major differences. In particular, if you were trained as a market researcher, you have to knowingly reprogram yourself to change what you look for, where you look for it, what you can expect to get, and how to analyze it.

Jane: Just from looking at this, it seems that CI is less precise than market research, right?

John: No. But CI often deals with forecasts or projections, where there is always uncertainty. The uncertainty lies in the underlying data, not in the tools for analysis or the analyst. The analyst does, however, have to be honest about any uncertainty in her prediction. Fake certainty eventually will destroy the analyst's credibility.

Identifying the CI You Need

How Do You Identify the CI That You REALLY Need?

- Start with what you *think* you know
  - What are they doing now?
  - What did they do last year?
  - Who is in charge?
- Are you certain that you *really* know it?
  - Are you just assuming it?
  - Are you relying on the past, on old data and impressions, and not on current data?
- Then distinguish between **what you need to know** and **what is just nice to know**:
  - If you had the CI you say you want right now, what decision could you make, and what action could you take, that you cannot do now?
- If you cannot answer that, maybe you need something else!

John: Now, since you are your own CI customer, at least in part, you have to learn how to figure out what you should be looking for. These points are proven aids to that. The last one is sort of a commandment in CI—there is a critical difference between need to know and nice to know. CI supports the need to know; using your time and effort to generate nice to know information is just wasting your time.

Jane: Don't we need to start with who are our real competitors?

John: Yes, but here you should at least list who you think your competitors are—You will fine tune that list as you go on.

I Need to Know...

- Who my competitors *really* are
- My competitors' current prices, pricing strategy, and pricing tactics
- My competitors' view of the market
- My competitors' ability and willingness to change
- How my competitors see my firm!

John: Now, for you, here is a starting point for doing your work on this new restaurant project.

Jane: Don't we also care about what kind of cuisine they offer? You know, what is on the menu?

John: Now you are starting to drift over into market research. Depending on what your restaurant is going to do, you may not even consider certain restaurants as competitors, regardless of cuisine. I mean, if you are going to have an oriental fine-dining facility, do you consider a take-out Chinese restaurant as a competitor? Your competitors may be better defined by where they are, and what kind of Clientele they attract. You know, like your possible investment, they are likely to be near the arts center, and work at getting subscribers to the local orchestra that performs there. And are those the kind of customers you want?

Let's take another approach. Here is a part of our checklist on finding out what specific CI you need on a regular basis.

Diagnostic Checklist—What CI You May Need

1. Identify potential new threats—Can CI help? What kinds of CI will help?
2. Identify recurring threats, internal and external—Can CI help? What kinds?

3. Could CI have helped you in the past? Look at past (avoidable) recent
   failures in
   i. marketing
   ii. acquisition/divestitures
   iii. sales performance
   iv. product development
   v. unexpected competitor successes

John: Got it? This is something to go over with your partners. In your case, "product development" is actually the development of a restaurant's concept.

Ok, let's look at the last slide in the deck.

How to Locate and Develop Critical Data

- Keep it clean—Be legal and ethical
  - You may get less data, but not a lot less
  - You also will be able to sleep at night
- Always keep in mind and separate what you know from what you suspect and what you just assume
  - For example, are their suppliers so powerful that they are setting the retail prices?

John: This last slide is a quick reminder about the need to stay ethical and to separate your preconceptions, and those of others, from facts. Now, let's talk about what you think you need to do and how you will go about doing it.

Jane: What if I just go to one of these restaurants and start looking around?

John: Please, think through what you need to know first. How about this? You make up a short checklist of what you want to do. Then make one visit, and Carolyn and I can go over how well it went.

Jane: OK.

Two weeks later we heard from Jane.

Jane: I've spoken with the partners about what they are planning to do. They are committed to changing the format of the new restaurant to "New American Casual" across all meals. They are looking to attract young professionals, who they feel are willing to pay a little more for fine food. They want to serve lunch and dinner, with a buffet on Sunday. We will have three major competitors, operating restaurants, all right around us—that is, around the new restaurant we are looking at, if we go forward with the investment and overhaul. We see them as going after the same customer base we are interested in. Here are some of the questions I have come up with for each one:

1. What percentage of their business is done on Friday and Saturday nights?
2. Do they have a similar menu or are they also planning to change to New American?
3. Have they tried anything like that in the past? What happened?
4. Do they offer a Sunday buffet? How well do they do? Have they ever offered one in the past? How well did that do?
5. How busy are they for lunch on Sunday?
6. What kind of customers do they aim for: young urban families with children, suburban couples in town for a concert, singles? Do they get what they are aiming for?
7. How profitable are they? If that is not available, how much business do they do on, say, Tuesday lunch, Wednesday evening, and Saturday evening? That is, how many covers?
8. What price point(s) do they aim for—that is, how much is the average appetizer, entrée, and dessert? Do most customers go for the high end or are they more frugal?
9. With respect to marketing, what do they advertise and feature: menu items, price, special events, links with concerts, identity of the chef, type of cuisine?
10. Do they have any customer retention/reward programs? Do customers seem to be using that?

John: This is a good start. Before I have you work with Carolyn on how to get this intelligence, let's go over your targeting and see which questions will generate actionable intelligence. Or to put it more simply, which questions have answers that are "need to know," and which are just "nice to know." In competitive intelligence, you aim for the first, that is, getting intelligence that you need to make your decision or to take a step. OK?

I will take them by number. So, for Number 1, on their Friday and Saturday night business volume, what decision could you, and your associates, make that you cannot make now?

Jane: It would tell us how much they will try to compete with us since we are going to stress that. In fact, we are considering initially doing only lunch daily, and a Sunday buffet. Then we might roll out dinner on Friday and Saturday nights, and then later expand dinner to the rest of the week. But, if these three restaurants, that is, the nearby competitors, do most of their business on Friday and Saturday, we might have to really prepare a hard launch because they will fight back if these nights are critical to them.

John: That sounds fine. What about Number 2, their menus and possible change?

Jane: Well, we are all very committed to the New American Casual format.

John: So whether or not the competing restaurant you are looking at did it in the past is not really critical, right? That is the aim of Number 3.

Jane: Right, but we want to know what their menu looks like so we can make sure that we can differentiate ourselves from them. And, if we are going to go head-to-head on an item, how are they doing it and pricing it?

John: Fine. Now Number 3 is out, but Number 2 is ok, at least in part. Now, we already know that they do not offer a Sunday buffet, but only holiday buffets. Do you really need to know what they did in the past? If so, how far back?

Jane: No, I guess this is more "nice to know."

John: That does not mean you should not collect it. Just don't spend your limited time and effort to collect it at the expense of collecting other, critical, intelligence.

Now, Number 5. That is something else we already know. They do not serve, usually, on Sundays. Why is it even on the list?

Jane: Frankly, one of the partners is not really deeply involved so far. He raised the question, so I guess he did not read the brief on the potential investment.

John: In the future, you have to make sure that you and your team are well educated on a project so you can be better clients. What would you think if that partner hired a firm to do that and tasked it with this question? Don't answer: it would be a waste of their time—and your money.

Now Number 6. Why?

Jane: We are going to aim at young urban singles and couples in town for a concert or some other event. So, we want to know who is our closest competition for that group.

John: If there is one, you should be regularly monitoring it once you are in business, right? Now, Number 7?

Jane: I am not sure. Maybe they want to know how hard they will compete, that is, will they cut prices sharply, with specials, etc.? Or is that something they cannot afford to do?

John: You should probably go back and discuss this question with them. What actions will they take depending on what the answers are? It sounds very much to be a "nice to know" question, but maybe there is more to it. You have to find that out.

Jane: Number 8 is very, very important. We are seeking to go to the upper end, so we need to know how much space there is between us and these competitors. What I mean is that we do not want to have so much daylight between us and them that we look, well, unaffordable, the kind of place you go once a year, that sort of thing.

As for Number 9, we are using their experience to see where we can go against them, where we may have to go to avoid going head-to-head, and, by comparing their menu with their marketing, to see what kinds of marketing works for the kinds of customers we are seeking.

John: Explain that a little more.

Jane: Well, for example, if a restaurant is linked with concerts and other events, how close is that link? Is it one we should work to establish? Do we even care about special events, like participating in the local jazz fest? The partners do not see that as our thing, so they feel we should not waste money advertising and promotion in that way.

John: Now, on customer rewards/retention programs, Number 10—What nugget are you looking for here?

Jane: We are thinking of offering one, a program that is. But, if there is one already in place, we look like a copycat, and we want to be a leader, not a follower.

John: What if they all have such programs?

Jane: I don't know. We have not thought about that. I think we might steer away completely just to look different, higher class.

John: So Number 10 could drive a key decision, right?

Jane: Yes.

John: OK, redo this list and get it to Carolyn before you both talk about approaches and likelihood of success.

Jane: Likelihood of success? What do you mean?

John: I mean, once you have your questions, which you are working on, and your targets, which you already know, you should evaluate just how likely it is that you will be able to get everything you want and need. If you do not like the odds, then it is a good time to rethink what you are looking for and revise it to aim at data that is more likely to be available and so you will be more able to develop the intelligence you need.

Jane emailed Carolyn later that day:

Carolyn—Here are my intelligence research questions, which I revised after talking with John:

1. What percentage of the competitors' business is done on Friday and Saturday nights?
2. Do they have a menu like a New American Casual menu?
3. What kind of customers do they aim for: young urban families with children, suburban couples in town for a concert, singles? Do they get what they aim for?
4. How much business do they do on, say, Tuesday lunch, Wednesday evening, and Saturday evening? That is, how many covers?
5. What price point(s) do they aim for? That is, how much is the average appetizer, entrée, and dessert? Do customers go for the high end or are they more frugal?
6. With respect to marketing—what do they advertise and feature? That is, menu items, price, special events, links with concerts, identity of the chef, and type of cuisine.
7. Do they have any customer retention/reward programs? Do customers seem to be using that?

I will call and we can talk about how to go about this.

Jane

One day later, Carolyn and Jane were able to connect:

Jane: Carolyn, have you had a chance to look at the list I sent yesterday? John went over it with me and we cut out some questions which we decided were not "need to know." Now, can we talk about how to get the rest answered?

Carolyn: Sure. I have the list in front of me. My first question to you is whether or not you have had any experience in working in or managing a restaurant?

Jane: None, no not really. Why?

Carolyn: Because one of the keys to developing CI is to know where the data you are looking for is developed, by whom, and where it moves. There are several reasons for that. First, it is hard to develop CI on subjects that your target does not care about or has not focused on. It is not impossible, but it can be very hard and costly. So, if you take question 7, what if one of the targets has such a program but only does it "because everyone else does it"? If they do not know if it works because they do not care about it, how can you then figure that out?

Jane: Well, I could ask people leaving a restaurant about it, or ask the staff what they think of it. At least I would have something.

Carolyn: Very good approach. Nice. So, let's hear how you might approach each of these. Number 1?

Jane: I guess that I could go there on a couple of nights, count the number of customers, and tabulate that?

Carolyn: Yes, but to be safe, you have to do that several times, so your statistics are valid, that is, based on a good sample. Also, you might try to chat up the receptionist once you are sort of a regular. Also, don't forget there is a bar—bartenders watch volume and that sort of thing—volume drives their tips. So, you should talk with them. Number 2?

Jane: Can I take a photo of the menu with my smart phone?

Carolyn: First, try asking for a menu you can keep—very often these non-chain restaurants will have a call-in menu that is the same or at least quite similar to their master menu. Taking a picture is quick, but sort of obvious. But if they do something like posting the daily specials on a board, it may be unavoidable.

For Number 3, I assume on-site observation is the key, right? And don't forget to review their advertising, which you will have to do for another point. Where and when they advertise may provide a little guidance here.

Jane: Yes. And Number 5 is also observation and an analysis of the menu—or menus, if they differ for different meals.

Carolyn: Don't forget to ask your server: what do people really like here, that sort of thing. Number 6 is pretty clear, right—get back access to issues of newspapers, local magazines, listen to local radio and TV, walk past the restaurant several weeks, and see what is posted.

Jane: Local magazines? Do they have one around here? I did not think that they did.

Carolyn: Never assume that possible data sources are unavailable. Always check. And, to get more information, research past restaurant reviews in the local print media.

Jane: What about digital media?

Carolyn: That's ok, but there is a lot of question how valid some online 5 star and no-star reviews by customers really are—or if they are really even written by customers. But, in any case, really work your way, carefully and slowly, through the competitor's website. And check past versions of the site that have been cached to look for critical changes over time.

Jane: How can I do that?

Carolyn: Use the Internet Archive—the Wayback Machine, at https://archive.org/web/.

Jane: As for Number 7, I can just ask when I go.

Carolyn: Also, record how and how often they contact you. Again, chat up the server. Now, on that, you are going to have to go several times, so you are going to become a local regular. But if all you do is ask questions every time you go, you will quickly stand out. You do not want that.

Jane: What are my options?

Carolyn: First, always prioritize your questions—determine which are the most critical and probably cannot be answered through your secondary research. Get them done first, in case you find your on-site data gathering efforts get cut short for some reason. Second, have other people go there too, but not acting like they are TV cops at a crime scene. The best questions are general, open-ended ones where you or your friends let someone "help."

Now, let's talk about how successful you think you can be on each of these. Develop for yourself a percentage of how well you think you and others can do to get the data and develop the intelligence you have identified. Make sure your odds are pretty good or change the questions and/or what you will do to get the data to improve your chance of answering them.

Jane, let's go out to lunch today to one of the targets and then to the local restaurant supply house. We are looking to see how each restaurant is spending its money when it comes to the things that customers actually see—the things that make up the ambiance. As customers, we don't see the kitchen in the restaurant; we just see the dining area. We see what they want us to see. You and I want to figure out about how much money they are putting into that. Every food-oriented business has to be investing back into that business to avoid getting stale or out of date or letting equipment lose its state-of-the-art status. Even with well-planned ambiance, what is popular in the decorating world today is terrible tomorrow. It seems likes colors change weekly.

So, when we have lunch we will each order different items and compare them. We will also be checking the utensils and plating, glassware, and linens. We will check out the ladies' room and the bar menu even if we just have nonalcoholic drinks. Hopefully, there will be a menu for carry-out food we can pick up.

Jane: Why linens?

Carolyn: In terms of linens, this where the owner or decorator, if there is one, takes over completely. They usually have a vision in their head of how the dining area should look. What colors should be there, what pictures should be on the wall, what feeling the dining room should evoke in the customers. Essentially, the owners of the restaurant are creating an ambiance with everything they are doing, from the flooring to the paint to the tableware. The menu and the food is just a part of it. Pricing that is tough, but we can give it a try.

That is why all of this is part of your CI. If it were as easy as going into their restaurant and eating a couple of meals, everybody would be doing it. Your job is not just to see what is there, but to see it through the eyes of your competitors and then understand what it means.

Later that day, we reviewed the project:

Carolyn: OK John, the lunch was good. Jane and I both enjoyed the food. We had different things. The menu was both a bit creative; it also had some items you would expect, cheeseburgers, club sandwiches, and so on. All in all, it's a nice comfortable place to eat lunch. We both enjoyed ourselves. The service was nice, being available without being too intrusive. We did have to wait a bit for the check. That makes we wonder about the staffing level. The plating and glassware were nice, nothing special. The ladies' room was clean, if a bit small. Our next step was to visit the restaurant supply store.

This is a beautiful restaurant supply store. It is nice and big and seems to carry everything that would be needed to supply a new restaurant venture in the way of plating, utensils, pots, pans, cooking needs, linens, and so on. I think they carry pretty much everything except professional appliances, and they can probably direct you to the firms which sell the professional versions of these kinds of products.

We started with the eating utensils. The selection went from gaudy to plain in terms of pattern and light to heavy in terms of weight. Now, studies have shown that people see more value in a plain, heavy piece of cutlery than they do in an ornate, lighter weight piece of cutlery. This does not hold true for glassware.

There, people are looking for a comfortable glass. They want a glass that is not too heavy and not too light, it can't be too round and it can't be too thin. It must be just right. Knowing that kind of information is a part of seeing through the competitor's eyes. We looked at the prices for them, so we could compare them with what the targets have and learn more about how the competitors approached their customers.

For example, in terms of plates, the chef at the first one likes stark white so he/she can show off the beautiful food and I don't blame them. When food looks beautiful, it tastes even better. This is true no matter what it is. We then priced the white plates being used.

I think Jane learned how thorough you have to be from our exercise.

What new problems did we run into with the client and how did we solve them?

The first problem we ran into was with the client's perception and attention.

With respect to perception, as we earlier found, the partners had no real idea of the success and failure rate for new restaurants opened in the United States. Not only did they grossly overestimate the failure rate, they also thought that the failure rate for non-chain restaurants was considerably higher than for chains. And that was very wrong, too. The study we mentioned earlier demonstrated that the restaurant failure rate is closer to one out of four, or 26 percent, in the first year, with lower failure rates in subsequent years. Among franchised chains, the cumulative failure rate was 57 percent during the first three years and 61 percent for independent restaurants—only a 4 point difference. So, they were wrong about that, too.

As for attention, the first round of work with Jane quickly disclosed that at least one of the partners was not paying attention to whatever data and intelligence was being provided on the new project. That is very bad, and, frankly, very tough for an outsider to overcome. We briefed Jane, but she felt overwhelmed as a junior member of the team, and was reluctant to challenge that senior partner on his lack of focus.

What happened at the client after we were done? How successful were we?

Jane quickly developed into a capable CI researcher. She worked with the partners, whom she recruited to visit the potential competitors—except for the one who did not like "details." He always found a reason not to participate. They eventually visited, "as customers," all the restaurants, plus the one they were considering. She—and they—quickly learned that a key issue for their potential new restaurant was not what its cuisine would be.

Rather, it soon became apparent that none of the three competing restaurants had enough business to support them robustly, much less an excess that could be "harvested" by Casual Investors' planned new investment.

It turned out that the number of people, of all types, who supported all the restaurants in the same area was smaller than Casual Investors first believed. They had been led to believe, from the existing owners, that the injection of new funds would necessarily generate additional business from customers who were already out there. In fact, the opposite was true.

Talking with staff at all restaurants—including the one under consideration—indicated that the customer flow downtown had been declining steadily, if slowly, for over 7 years. For the new investment to succeed, Casual Investors not only would have to overhaul the restaurant but also would have to invest more time and more money in recruiting and then keeping new customers willing to come downtown. These were people who were not doing so now.

Casual Investors then did some simple research into the demographics of the area served by the competing restaurants and the one it is interested in. It found that the market was graying—that is, getting older—and that this older market was less and less interested in going downtown, even for events at the arts center. Casual Investors had indicated it was targeting a younger Clientele, but the size of that demographic group in this area seemed to be static or even declining.

Checking the nearby arts center's draw, it found that the center's ticket sales were relatively static, but with a slight decline over the past three years. Digging deeper, the company found that the arts center had actually reduced some of its ticket prices to drive up attendance, and that its portfolio of events was now primarily aimed at families with small children. In other words, the "big local draw" was not drawing the kind of customers Casual Investors was seeking, and was, in fact, having its own trouble drawing, profitable customers.

Following these efforts, Casual Investors called off the negotiations. Jane, thanks to her efforts, was brought into Casual Investors as a junior partner and tasked with providing CI on all future purchases and investments, which the partners agreed was now to be a baseline requirement.

We were pleased to hear that when Jane contacted us. She asked for some help: how can she learn to write up what she finds for everyone's use. So, we gave her a short note on this:

Quick Tips on Writing Up CI Analyses

One, despite the existence of very good voice recognition packages, writing is still very different from speaking. Those differences may be diminishing, but they still exist simply because, in writing, your audience cannot hear your inflection, your emphasis, and the concepts or words you vocally stress.

So, spend enough time on your writing. First drafts should be just that—drafts that are to be improved by reviewing and rewriting them.

Two, remember that anything that you write down might have to be read in the future by someone who cannot talk to you. If you are writing it for your own records, remember that when you read it again seven days, two months, or six months from now, you will not have at hand all the research that you did, nor will you have retained all the analytical nuances and insights that came out while you were analyzing that research. So always make the document complete. In other words, start with stating what it is you were researching, that is, the question or questions you were trying to answer. Then, answer each of them in turn, including the supporting research at that point.

Three, analysis is not the same as data. When writing up a report or file memo, consider keeping the two items separate. One way is to simply label your analysis as "analysis," "conclusion," "discussion," or the like. And then you can separate the supporting data from that heading. By doing this, you clearly communicate to the next reader where the data end and your personal analysis begins.

Four, keep it simple. A report is not an exercise designed to show how smart you are or how well you have mastered the English language, or some scientific or arcane subset of it. You are trying to communicate your research results with a clear message. Simple means be direct, not indirect. For example, in general, things do not happen. Events, people, or something else cause them to happen. Write your sentences that way.

Five, if you do not know something, or you could not answer a question, just say so. It is very deceptive to make it appear that your analysis or your memo is somehow a complete coverage of the topic when you know, and we all know, that the odds of it being complete are remote. For example, if you do not know the cause of some event (see point four above), say that.

Six, keep it short. From time to time, there may be reasons for you to detail or record all that you did not find, resources you could not utilize, or other such omissions. However, that is the exception rather than the rule. In addition to keeping the report short, keep your sentences short. As a rule, if you cannot read a sentence back aloud without taking a breath, it is too long. Cut it into two or even three shorter sentences.

Seven, remember that even if you will be the ultimate beneficiary, or the only beneficiary, of your intelligence research and analysis, write it up at some point. And do that write-up sooner rather than later. Why? Because you may have to refer to it one day and your memory is imperfect. What you so clearly remember as being the result of your research and analysis may not be exactly complete and correct. In fact, over time, it is almost guaranteed that your recollection will vary widely from reality. So, when you write up what you just found, write it up as if you were writing it up either (A) for a third person or

(B) for your own consumption. In either case, make sure that you indicate the sources of each key finding, at least in a shorthand way. Just listing a set of resources at the end ranging from a homepage, a LinkedIn profile, and Facebook page to telephone interviews and product samples is not enough. For you to make sense of your own analysis if there would be a question, you would have to redo the research. Your purpose here is to avoid doing that— to make your research useful to you in the future, and if necessary, defensible to those who might directly or indirectly challenge it.

Eight, if you are a note taker, save your work notes, at least for short time. Save them electronically, save them in a folder, but save at least the critical elements. There is usually no reason to keep these notes after a reasonable time, say 90 days, has passed. At that point, even if your research and analysis was complete and correct at the time, it is likely you would have to redo at least a part of it to bring it up-to-date. So, do not encumber yourself with unnecessary files and notes. Put a delete or destroy date on these to avoid being a data hoarder. No matter how much space you have in your computer drives, saving unnecessary files there merely makes it run all its own searches more slowly. Of course, if your firm has a document retention policy, learn it so you can abide by it.

LOOKING BACK ONE YEAR LATER

We contacted Jane about a year later to see how she and Casual Investors were doing. The firm was fully committed to using CI as a part of its "due diligence," the comprehensive appraisal of a business or investment undertaken by a prospective buyer or investor, to establish and evaluate its assets and liabilities and evaluate its commercial potential. Jane's work on a second potential investment had turned up some competitive weaknesses in the project, resulting in the firm changing the project from a passive minority investment to an acquisition and makeover.

During that year, the other partners bought out the partner who was not very detail-oriented. It turned out that his reluctance to get involved in "minor details like this intelligence," in his own words, was behind the preliminary targeting of the restaurant and of this new project. He had pushed it as being "really worthwhile, something we should move on, and move on now." Also, he objected to putting an ethics guide for CI in writing, which made some partners wonder about how he might do business in the future.

Casual Investors now approaches investments and other projects by doing a preliminary CI assessment on the target before even talking with its owners. It has also run CI assessments on its existing book of investments, resulting in the liquidation of one smaller minority investment. The results of these changes: the firm's losses have fallen and its rate of return is 15 percent higher than in the past.

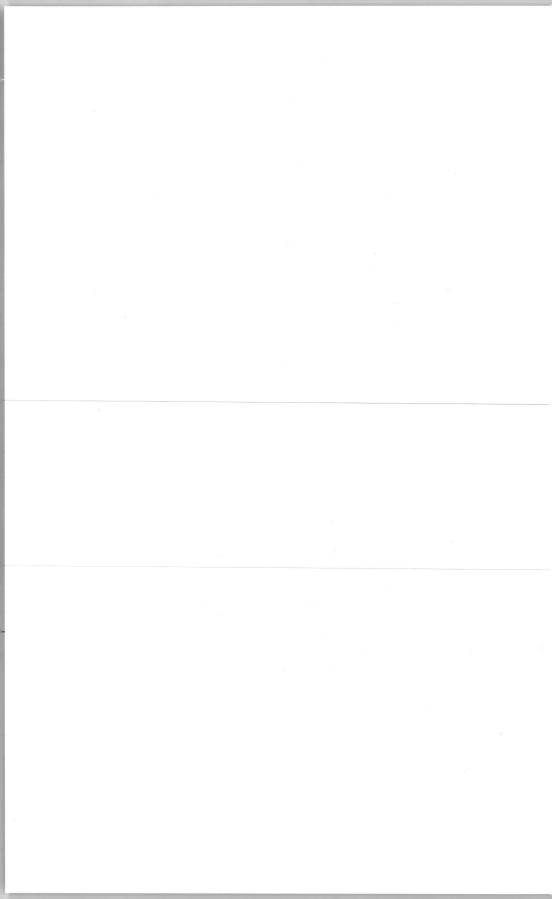

4

Creating a New CI Function and Staffing a New CI Team

THE CASE

About the Company

Egbertz Chemical is a new, $1+ billion, publicly traded industrial chemical company. It was created less than six months ago by a spin-off composed of the petrochemical and related industrial chemical assets of a much larger manufacturing, coatings, and chemicals company, Koatin. Koatin did this, it said, because it was seeking to focus more on what its management viewed as its "core markets." Egbertz's component businesses have been operating in the United States, Canada, and Latin America for almost 20 years.

Koatin retained no businesses in Egbertz's current market space. However, there are still some important connections. For example, Egbertz expects to continue to be the prime supplier of two chemical inputs for its former parent. However, these existing supply contracts with Koatin run out in one and two years, respectively. As of now, Egbertz has no indication what will happen to them after that time.

Its Management, Owners, and Employees

The personnel situation in some areas is now unstable. While the executives and managers operating Egbertz were with the predecessor's operations for 3–10 years, there is one exception: the president, Monica. Monica is not now the CEO.

She came to Egbertz during the spin-off from outside of Koatin. She was formerly executive vice president of a major competitor of Koatin's, but one which is not in Egbertz's current markets. However, the current CEO of Egbertz has indicated that she will retire in another six months or so, which triggered a search by its new board of directors for a successor. It is rumored that Monica is a serious candidate, but she is not the only one under consideration.

The president of Egbertz is a very direct person. She believes many meetings end up being a waste of time and is not hesitant to make that clear:

> I want people to talk to each other and not hide behind thing like overheads and buzz words. If I had my way, we would stop the use of acronyms. After a while people forget what they stand for. And industry slang is not far behind in hiding facts and evading responsibilities. Put that together with leaderless teams and you end up with soft decision making without anyone taking responsibility. If I have to make a decision, I want you to give me a one- or two-page summary of the issues, a list of the available options, your recommendation, and I will sign off on it. If you cannot tell me what is going on in two pages, come back to me when you can.

For the moment, Egbertz does not have its own legal team. It is relying on outside legal counsel, but Monica wants to build up that internal capability quickly. In the interim, she has directed that staff call on the outside law firm only for "vital" matters. Other personnel issues facing the firm are in research and development (R&D) and in CI (see below).

A Look at Its Competitive Environment and Market Profile

The market that Egbertz is entering includes competitors that are largely similarly positioned firms. Three of these competing firms are independent, and one is a subsidiary of an industrial coatings firm. The fifth firm is owned by a Saudi Arabian investment trust, which acquired it 18 months ago. The sixth, the last, is owned by an oil refining company, in turn partially and indirectly owned by the Russian government. All six competitors, as well as Egbertz, regard this as a commodity market. Our research and Koatin's own past experiences indicate that they all currently compete on that basis.

What were its plans? What is coming next?

Egbertz's current situation is not yet stabilized. For example, the R&D supporting what is now Egbertz had been conducted by Koatin in the past. Koatin retained virtually all these individuals and all its other R&D activities and assets in the spin-off. Koatin reportedly kept the R&D assets because its management felt it could not afford to lose the expertise of these people even though the spin-off meant that it was now out of Egbertz's particular market.

That means that Egbertz currently has no R&D team of its own. Egbertz is trying to deal with that quickly, too. Unfortunately, since it cannot recruit from its old parent, under the terms of the agreement governing the spin-off, this process will take some time.

Status of Intelligence Operations

The CI situation is similarly in flux. Egbertz, in the spin-off, was assigned three members of the former parent company's CI team, who are now in place there. Koatin's CI team operated only at the corporate level, developing strategic intelligence and supporting the annual plan, corporate development, and the investment plan. At Koatin, CI reported to the director of strategic planning. Before the spin-off, no CI staff members were imbedded with or directly supported any of the business units that make up what is now Egbertz.

At Egbertz, CI now reports directly to the president. The reason is that the new president sees her intelligence needs as immediate and primarily strategic. But, as with other aspects of the spin-off, that will also be changing. The head of CI, Will, has recently announced he will retire in a few months. The other two members of the CI team have applied to transfer to the firm's emerging strategic planning team. Given their experience in supporting strategic planning at the former parent, that transfer has been approved, and will go forward, probably before their CI replacements are in place.

What problems/issues were identified by the client?
Monica told us that

> I think we definitely have to have an intelligence capability. We have six major competitors, all of which are large. And two of them are not even U.S.-based, although they also serve the U.S. market, our largest market.

> I think that the intelligence here should be aimed at the overall strategies of our competitors. That is the way it was done at Koatin, and how we also did it at my old firm.

> In addition, I have some concerns about how deep we should go with more tactical intelligence. Let me explain.

> This industry is very concentrated. There are only seven firms in it in the U.S. Frankly, it is my expectation that the company owned, indirectly, by the Russians will pull out, in part due to economic issues in Russia. Also, suspect that the one owned by a coatings firm that is competing directly with Koatin will either be closed or spun off, as it is relatively a very small player. It is not in very good shape, and this market is one that depends on scale. The net result is that, within a couple of years, this market will probably be even more concentrated than it is now.

> And we are in an odd position because we have to decide if we want to build up our own research and development. Or outsource it to Koatin—although that option is pretty much off the table now—or work with a competitor in this area. In fact, there is talk about some of the U.S.-based competitors creating

an independent research and development center which we would all fund. In any case, all the remaining players could end up a lot closer. And frankly I am uncomfortable with having us conduct tactical intelligence against what could be research & development partners who are also competitors.

Also, there may a legal issue with that. What I mean is that, if we end up with four big competitors in this U.S. market space, we have something very close to an oligopoly, a market dominated by a few big firms. And the U.S. antitrust laws forbid price or market cooperation. In fact, we would probably have to get U.S. government approval for the proposed research and development center before we could set it up. While I cannot speak for the other firms, I personally would not move forward without such approval.

Anyway, because of these circumstances, our outside lawyers have warned us to stay away from any activities that would involve collecting price and related intelligence, such as on pricing and credit policies, because that could potentially expose us to additional antitrust scrutiny.

OUR PERSPECTIVES

Key Diagnostic Quiz Results

How is Egbertz's intelligence team staffed, trained, and managed?
Egbertz's current intelligence team will be entirely replaced in the very near future.

Yes
The new strategic intelligence team is expected to have specific training on strategic intelligence.

The new strategic intelligence team is expected to have some experience in developing and providing strategic intelligence.

The new strategic intelligence team is expected to have good written and oral communication skills.

Those responsible for strategic intelligence activities will clearly understand its objectives, target audience, and expected measures of success.

The new strategic intelligence team is expected to have a clear understanding of who its internal end users/customers are.

The training to be provided for members of the new strategic intelligence team dealing with collecting primary information should include techniques such as selecting the appropriate people to contact, conducting both telephone and face-to-face interviewing, developing and making effective use of internal and external networks, developing and making effective use of external networks, and working trade shows and industry meetings.

Maybe/Perhaps

The new strategic team is expected to have some current industry knowledge.

No

The current intelligence team has no process in place to train interested and appropriate personnel in the skills and tools necessary to collect secondary information, or in the skills and tools necessary to collect primary information.

The current CI team does not have a process to train interested and appropriate personnel in the skills and tools necessary to analyze and then disseminate information to appropriate end users.

How does Egbertz's team get its direction on targets, on its data collection, and on deliverables?

Egbertz's current CI team will be entirely replaced in the very near future.

Yes

The current CI program meets its users' needs on an ongoing basis.

The new CI team is expected to provide strategic intelligence reports and assessments on our competitors and/or emerging threats they believe are most important.

The new CI team will have a systematic process for identifying and defining its intelligence needs.

The new CI team will use both primary and secondary intelligence sources.

The firm's CI activities will have a set of clearly defined objectives, with clearly identified end users.

Maybe/Perhaps

The new CI team may have specific criteria to decide what types of data are to be collected and which competitors it will be collected on.

No

The new CI team will not focus its intelligence efforts on products/technologies and other tactical targets.

Business/program/product/technology managers are not responsible for providing some of their own CI.

Where does the CI team get its data?

Egbertz's current CI team will be entirely replaced in the very near future.

Yes

The current CI team uses secondary sources of information (public materials, analysts' reports, etc.) to learn about key competitors.

The current CI team and the new CI team both use management's strategic intelligence requirements to guide collection.

Maybe/Perhaps

The current CI team may use primary/human sources of intelligence in addition to secondary sources.

No

There are no indications whether the current CI team has developed and uses both internal and external networks to assist in its data gathering.

There are no indications whether employees all report information about competitors or relevant emerging threats and opportunities to the appropriate managers.

The current CI team has not established a set of legal and ethical guidelines covering the gathering, use, and communication of CI.

What intelligence does the CI team provide?

Egbertz's current CI team will be entirely replaced in the very near future.

Yes

The current CI team prepares profiles of Egbertz's competitors; the new strategic intelligence team will focus on strategic issues, possibly including early warning.

The current intelligence program systematically collects, analyzes, and disseminates intelligence to those people in the firm responsible for business planning and decision making.

The new strategic intelligence team will provide trend analyses to determine potential new forces in the firm's business environment that other parts of the firm, focused on performing their daily functions, might not be aware of.

What does Egbertz do to help its intelligence process?

Egbertz's current CI team will be entirely replaced in the very near future.

Yes

Egbertz's management is making visible efforts both to support and to use intelligence.

The firm recognizes strategic intelligence as a legitimate and necessary activity in today's marketplace.

Maybe/Perhaps

There is no indication one way or other that employees, at all levels in the firm, understand and support the importance of and the firm's commitment to CI.

No

Egbertz does not have a formal set of legal and ethical guidelines designed specifically for intelligence.

There is no legal department in place to regularly review organized intelligence activities, as well as any DIY CI activities, to ensure that they are being conducted legally and ethically.

The firm does not provide education on ethics and legalities of CI to all employees involved in any intelligence activities, even to DIYers and others outside of the CI team or individual.

What do Egbertz's managers and executives expect from and get from the CI team?

Egbertz's current CI team will be entirely replaced in the very near future. It has not been in place long enough to have any track record.

Yes

The strategic intelligence program will be run by a small group of people, professionally trained to produce CI for the management unit's varying needs, including business planning and decision making.

Maybe/Perhaps

Senior management is willing to hear things that they might not want to hear from the CI team or individual.

What results has the CI process achieved at the firm?

Egbertz's current CI team will be entirely replaced in the very near future. It has not been in place long enough to have any track record.

What were the real problems there? Why are they different from what the company said they were?

While the client is focused on rebuilding the CI team, there are other issues involved with that team, which need to be dealt with. The client is looking to adapt or clean up what they have, or more accurately, what it inherited. Instead of that, it should take the opportunity, as it is doing with research & development (remember the client does not like acronyms like R&D), to start with a clean slate. Here are the four major problems that we soon identified:

1. The current president is seeking to become CEO. If she does not get that job and leaves, all the work she is trying to do with respect to the CI team could be lost. The client will be worse off there than it is now because it will be without any CI capabilities within a few months.

2. Egbertz does not have a mission statement for its CI team reflecting the realities of its new position and existing market. In fact, we have yet to find a copy of any current statement. For example, should it get involved with "early warning" activities? The client should decide on that before beginning to hire a new CI team.

3. The president has too narrow a view of what CI can legally do vis-à-vis its competitors. The client may need to reconsider the scope of the CI team's work before moving forward.

4. The client has no job description for what will be an entirely new set of CI team members who need to hit the ground running.

Problem 1—Position of Sponsor

To deal with the potentially confusing situation facing Egbertz, we decided to work as if the current president would become the CEO. As a consultant, you must deal with things as they are, not as you would like them to be. Realistically, if the current president were not named as CEO, it was highly likely that she would quickly move on, causing, as we noted, several problems.

However, recognizing the flux at the CEO level and the pending transfer or retirement of the entire three-person CI team, we elected to develop and help the client put in place policies and job descriptions that were only tentative. That is, they were solid enough to be used at once, which was vital. Competitors do not stop competing just because your CI team is not in place.

The status of this work required an acknowledgement from the client that these documents and policies would have to be finalized once the CEO and CI team situations were clarified. Fortunately, we were able to raise the issue of the long-term scope of work of the new CI team without having the individuals in place yet.

Also, by not driving to finalize these products and procedures, we did not use up the limited and valuable time of the soon-to-depart CI team. But the personnel transformation process had already started, to be completed once the CEO situation was resolved and the CI recruiting was completed. No one's hands were tied, but all involved, including those to join later, were alerted to the fact that things were necessarily still under development.

As it turned out, Monica was soon named as CEO and asked to serve as both CEO and president of Egbertz. That "solved" one part of the problem.

Problems 2 and 4—Lack of Mission Statement and Job Description

Developing a mission statement is a vital predicate to developing job descriptions for the entirely new CI team to be hired during the next few months. We had to remember to suggest that the final mission statement for this clearly keeps the new CI team away from price and pricing, even though, as we noted, that is a much too narrow reading of the law.

But, given the legal concerns hinted at by the president, we probed to see if she would be ok with having the firm's internal lawyers, once hired, review the mission statement. That not only would give her a greater level of comfort but also would bring the new legal team into the CI process at a very early stage, a very good start for them and for the new CI team as well.

That kind of involvement by a legal team is critical to the success of every CI team, but in this case, it was particularly important. That is because were dealing with a variety of moving pieces, particularly in personnel. It is a lot to expect that an entirely new CI team would have to start by drafting a mission statement the day the new members arrived. Also, the client could not present them with a job description if no one in authority has yet decided on what direction the CI unit would, and would not, take.

Strategic Intelligence Issues

We started by making an outline of what we thought the client should focus:

Strategic Intelligence Issues for Egbertz—Confidential

1. Targeting
   a. Determine Egbertz's competitors—now and in the future.
      i. Start with client's own list.
      ii. Who do its customers regard as competitors?
      iii. Who do industry observers see as competitors?
      iv. Who are potential entrants? Most often they come from suppliers and joint venture partners.
      v. Winnow that list into priorities of which are to be tracked.
         1. Every day
         2. Every month
         3. Every quarter or longer
   b. Deal with long-term, strategic issues.
      i. What is a long-term time horizon? One year? Five years?
      ii. Set up early warning program? That program would focus on key trends and forces shaping the industry and facing competitors.
         1. They may not be the same.
         2. It requires patience and significant time commitment.
         3. Can generate major payoff—Note Shell Oil Company's work here.
   c. There is to be no direct contact with targets.
   d. Also, no focus on pricing data.
   e. Create and monitor "war" games?
2. Reporting
   a. Direct report to:
      i. CEO?
      ii. COO/president?
   b. Supports "C" level officers—direct access as needed?
   c. Supports board of directors—direct access on quarterly basis?
   d. Aids strategy development, business development, risk management, and investment teams as needed?

3. Evaluation
   a. Evaluation of long-term strategic intelligence is harder than evaluation of short-term, tactical intelligence.
      i. Longer wait time to see if forecasts are correct.
      ii. Actions by Egbertz taken in response to CI can change what competitors do from what was forecast.
      iii. In either case, need honest end user feedback on regular basis—separate from regular personnel evaluations.
   b. Early warning is very hard to evaluate, but critical to supporting long-term thinking and planning.
4. Legal issues/compliance
   a. Get mission statement reviewed by legal department once it is on site.
   b. Train legal department on intelligence—makes them better counselors.
      i. Get them to join in "war" games?
         1. Helps them understand intelligence better.
         2. Adds different perspective to sessions.
      ii. Legal department can also be useful partner in getting documents and data from governments and law suits.

Carolyn: We better explain the term "war games" to Monica and her team—they might not be familiar with the concept.

John: How is this? Business war gaming simulates competitive moves and countermoves in a business setting. The games are usually set in the present and the near future. Executives and managers role play what might happen if there are specific changes in the competitive environment or in competitors' actions. They role play their own firm as well as their competitors. Internal intelligence teams often provide the background on the competitors and suggest their potential actions and reactions.

Carolyn: OK. But there is something else. With the promotion of Monica to CEO, her time will soon become even more constrained. There is no way she or the CI team, now in the process of moving to new jobs, would be able to get involved to this level of detail.

We then decided to approach it through developing a mission statement, a working one, for the CI team, as well as an ethics statement and a job description, also working, to permit them to recruit needed new employees quickly.

Problem 3—Legal Issues with Respect to Scope of CI Team's Work

As we noted, the president has a very narrow view of how the antitrust laws might impact the operation of her CI team. We had a brief internal discussion on this:

John: Based on my background as an attorney, I think that what she said is a way too strict reading of the antitrust laws. CI is procompetitive, not anticompetitive. So, collecting price intelligence is OK, as long at the firms do not collude on pricing.

Carolyn: I know that and so does Monica—probably. But she is firm. I suspect that she is concerned that the number of competitors may implode—you know the way that has happened in many commodity markets under price pressures. So, it is better for her to be safer now. In addition, she is likely a victim of the "that's the way we do it" view of the world. And it is a view also held by the soon-to-depart CI team members as well as the current CEO and the rest of senior management.

So, we decided not to pursue this.

Where and how did we solve the client's real problems and help the client?

With problems 1 and 3 out of the way, we could focus on problems 2 and 4. Our job is to help get the client rolling with an effective strategic intelligence program that everyone will be comfortable with.

Mission Statement

We had previously asked to get a copy of the mission statement for the current CI team. While the team was in the process of leaving, we wanted to review the charter that the client inherited. Our idea was that, from an acceptance point of view, starting with the one they have may make it easier for Monica and the others at the client to accept the resulting mission statement for a new team. Giving the client an entirely new team, with a new charter, under a new president, with a new CEO in the works is a lot of change to deal with. We thought that at least we can make it feel less radical by starting with something that is familiar—its existing mission statement and then work from there.

After asking again, we soon received Egbertz's current mission statement and quickly saw that it was a very basic one, obviously created because "they had to have one." In fact, no one seemed to know where or when it had been developed. It said:

The mission of the intelligence unit is to:

1. maintain general intelligence awareness;
2. provide an input into planning; and
3. conduct special [by this they probably mean one-time] assignments.

Putting it diplomatically, this is a dreadful statement. A mission statement for a CI unit, or any intelligence team, should serve several purposes:

- First, it should identify why the unit exists and what the firm expects from it.
- Second, it can be an opportunity for the unit (particularly, if it is new) to affirmatively sell the concept of intelligence and its benefits to a wide audience, which should include more parties than its immediate clients.
- Third, it can be used to deal with potential image problems, related to the concept of "corporate spies" in an affirmative, even aggressive basis.

In addition, when possible, a mission statement could include something about having the end user use its work product, that is, requiring that the intelligence produced actually be utilized. However, that does not work well if the firm puts it only in the mission statement of the intelligence team. The better way is to make sure that the job descriptions of the intelligence team's internal clients also include language to the effect that they will include the intelligence provided to them in their decision making.

Given the weakness of the existing statement, we decided to work up a new mission statement and then get back to the client. However, while we could begin the drafting, the final version of any mission statement should be one worked out by the firm's CI unit with the firm's legal team. That process takes time, and here we had the entire CI team leaving in the very near future. So, as discussed, we settled on developing an interim mission statement for the team that the client can use this in recruiting and installing the new CI team.

It is important to label it as "interim." And we had to make sure that the client will have the new CI team, whomever it includes, quickly work with the new legal department, and with the top officer that they will report to, on updating this. Sometimes you have to deal with a landscape which is changing by building that change into your process.

Drafting a Mission Statement

We also wanted to make sure everyone in the firm knows what CI is, particularly the incoming legal team, which will eventually review this statement. Given the mission statement's added "educational" role, we also included something on having internal customers actually use the CI they ask for and get.

Interim Mission Statement—First Draft

Competitive Intelligence (CI) involves the use of public sources to develop data on competition, competitors, and the market environment. It then transforms, by analysis, that data into information. Public, in CI, means all information you can legally and ethically identify, locate, and then access.

The CI unit's mission is to develop and to communicate an in-depth and current understanding of the following to senior management on a regular and as-needed basis:

- Current and future products/services of major competitors.
- Current technologies underlying the activities of major competitors.
- Current market activities of major competitors.
- Current and future business strategies employed by major competitors.
- Identity of potential new competitors.

This competitive intelligence will be used by officers and managers of the corporation in setting overall business strategies and making decisions on marketing, manufacturing, and distribution tactics.

This first draft mission statement had several immediate issues. First, it was way too broad, since the CEO-to-be said that she wants the team to be strategically oriented. If the client wants to broaden it in the future, that is her decision; it is not our place as consultants to force that decision on them now. Second, the client, and presumably the new team, all already know what CI is. In addition, the issue of ethical behavior would be dealt with separately.

That quickly led to a second draft:

Interim Mission Statement—Second Draft

The CI unit's mission is to develop and to communicate an in-depth and current understanding of the following to senior management on a regular and as-needed basis:

- Future products/services of major competitors.
- Current technologies underlying the activities of major competitors.
- Current market activities of major competitors.
- Current and future business strategies employed by major competitors.
- Identity of potential new competitors.

This strategic competitive intelligence will be used by officers and managers of the corporation in setting overall business strategies and making related decisions on marketing, manufacturing, and distribution strategies.

In this situation, the internal customer or end user, as some call her, presumably here Monica as CEO, would still have to decide on whether or not to include the first point, "future products and services," as well as the second point, "current technologies," as targets of the intelligence team. But, given her previous comments, we then decided to eliminate both for now. They could always be added later.

The client will be told that it will need more than a statement in the CI mission statement that people have to use CI. It must understand that it must make equivalent changes in the job descriptions of these officers and managers, so that their performance will also be measured by how well they ask for and then use CI.

The final issues that we felt had to be dealt with were the DIYers, as well as educating employees on CI. We decided to add:

> The CI unit is also responsible for the design and execution of programs to train all employees about CI, including legal and ethical limits on the collection of data.

The client will be advised that an option is to add support for this additional mission to the legal department's mission statement as well. If it goes for this, it will add a lot to the CI process. Having the legal team onboard with CI, having it understand what CI is and is not, can generate powerful support for the entire CI program, particularly when others still have these concerns. It also helps to make better clients for the CI team. We have found that, when someone does not know about CI, they sometimes can try to pressure a CI team to do things that are not ethical. This connection between the CI team and legal team protects everyone.

However, since this statement touches on both end users and the legal team, we decided to reinsert the definition of CI:

Interim Mission Statement—Third Draft

Competitive Intelligence (CI) involves the use of public sources to develop data on competition, competitors, and the market environment. It then transforms, by analysis, that data into information. Public, in CI, means all information you can legally and ethically identify, locate, and then access.

The CI unit's mission is to develop and to communicate an in-depth and current understanding of the following to senior management on a regular and as-needed basis:

- Future products/services of major competitors.
- Current technologies underlying the activities of major competitors.
- Current and future business strategies employed by major competitors.
- Identity of potential new competitors.

This strategic competitive intelligence will be used by officers and managers of the corporation in setting overall business strategies and making related decisions on marketing, manufacturing, and distribution strategies.

The CI unit is also responsible, with the cooperation of the legal department, for the design and execution of programs to train all employees about CI, including legal and ethical limits on the collection of data.

We then reviewed this draft with Monica. With her position as the new CEO stabilized, we got a lot done quickly. First, after discussing the mission statement, she is even more firm that she wants the CI unit limited to strategic intelligence—only. So, she did not want any language about "future products/ services of competitors," but felt that some language about "plans and strategies for future products/services" should be added to the list. Second, she brought up "early warning" as a mission for the unit. We asked her to elaborate, since early warning means different things to different people.

To her, it means looking out beyond the next year or so, which is also her definition of strategic vision. More specifically, she saw the firm as in an industry that is subject to major forces outside of the routine changes in its market that all firms face.

Monica: In terms of early warning, I mean just that. We are heavily dependent on what happens in the petroleum industry and in its markets, especially with issues like pricing and supplies. And some of that can be overwhelming as well as coming up very quickly. The more we know to expect change and to deal with it, the safer we are.

I know that Shell has been doing this for years and it has helped them foresee how to handle major economic, environmental, and market changes—yes even political ones.

What I want is an outline of what the intelligence team, I would think it should have the name strategic intelligence, and not competitive intelligence, or perhaps strategic competitive intelligence—yes, that is better. Anyway, I want something more detailed about what the strategic intelligence team should be doing with respect to early warning. This is well beyond a mission statement. It is to be an action brief.

I know that Shell has dedicated many, many people to this for many years. We cannot and will not be able to do that. So, what can a three-person team do that will bring real value to us?

I think you should talk with Will, the current head of the CI team, before he retires, to get an idea of what he sees as feasible. Also, can you work with him to develop a description of the kind of experience, skills, and background we need for his replacement? I mean, I know I would want someone with years of experience in this industry doing intelligence work—but there are only a few of those, and frankly, I do not think that those outside of our shop are very good. So, we need some help and guidance there.

Also, I think that we have to have a clear policy on when we go outside for intelligence support and what these outside providers can and cannot do.

OK, so we need a little tweak on the mission statement, adding early warning and future product strategies. Also, based on what we have discussed, I want a separate action brief for the early warning program, and Helicon's help in developing a profile for recruitment. Got it?

We also made sure to avoid using an acronym for strategic intelligence in keeping with Monica's expressed policy. That produced the "final" interim mission statement:

Interim Mission Statement—Final Draft

Strategic Intelligence involves the use of public sources to develop data on competition, competitors, and the market environment. It then transforms, by analysis, that data into information. Public, in strategic intelligence, means all information you can legally and ethically identify, locate, and then access.

The Strategic Intelligence Unit's mission is to develop and to communicate an in-depth and current understanding of the following to senior management on a regular and as-needed basis:

- Plans and strategies for future products/services.
- Current technologies underlying the activities of major competitors.
- Current and future business strategies employed by major competitors.
- Identity of potential new competitors.
- Early warning of major economic, environmental, market, and political changes impacting the firm's businesses.

This strategic intelligence will be used by officers and managers of the corporation in setting overall business strategies and making related decisions on marketing, manufacturing, and distribution strategies.

The strategic intelligence unit is also responsible, with the cooperation of the legal department, for the design and execution of programs to train all employees about strategic intelligence, including legal and ethical limits on the collection of data.

From there, we moved to developing an ethics statement, working with the current head of the CI—soon to be strategic intelligence—team. Following that, we would move to work on the early warning "brief" while the current CI team leader would work with us to write the job description. In each case, our job was to facilitate and work the client through the process. In some cases, there is more hands-on work than in others.

Ethics Statement

We started by asking the head of CI, Will, if Egbertz had any policy that dealt with, or even touched on, developing intelligence. His answer was very direct:

> **Will:**   No, not really. We do have one on price fixing that bars us from talking about pricing with competitors and another with handling trade secrets that someone may try to sell us. Do we really need more than that? I mean by focusing on strategy aren't we already out of that arena?

Our response is that the firm should have one. There are positive benefits to having an ethical policy that applies to how the intelligence unit operates. For example, by developing a statement of ethical standards to supplement legal ones, management sends a clear message to its employees that the company expects more from them than the bare minimum of "Don't break the law."

Also, an ethical statement provides an external measuring stick. That is, if your firm is hiring an outside intelligence consultant, you should ask that the firm be bound by your own standards. If the contractor has its own standards—or uses SCIP's (Strategic and Competitive Intelligence Professionals) "Code of Ethics for CI Professionals"—then having your own set of written standards enables you to ask the potential contractor to discuss its these standards with you and compare the fit, or lack of fit, with yours.

The best ethics policies are those that are drafted in cooperation with the legal department, which are simple and direct, provide guidance, and do not merely tell people in doubt to contact someone. They also should reflect a firm's unique situation and competitive environment. However, since the client will be dealing with a 100 percent turnover of the entire intelligence team, it needs an interim policy in place now. That, along with the interim mission statement, should later be revised by the new intelligence team, in cooperation with the new legal department, after each new team gets grounded.

Drafting an Ethics Statement

We began the process by asking the client to start. Will offered to start with "a pretty good policy that I am familiar with." He emailed us what he had to start a telephone discussion:

Will: I got the following from a friend, and tried to rework it so it was not so formal and preachy.

I numbered the sections so we could discuss them. Sorry that we cannot meet, but I am transitioning faster than I thought and my schedule is a mess.

1. Competitive information is a valuable tool that allows us to understand and manage our markets, products, and services so we can better meet our customers' needs. However, we must gather and use that information properly.

2. It is important that we comply with the law in acquiring information, which prohibits theft, blackmail, wiretapping, electronic eavesdropping, bribery, improper inducement, receiving stolen property, threats, and other improper methods.

3. It is important that we acquire information ethically. We must not misrepresent who we are or who we work for.

4. We will also respect the confidentiality of our competitors' and suppliers' information. We will not use information another company has marked "proprietary" or "confidential," regardless of how it was obtained, unless the owner gives us the material for a specific purpose or the material has become public information. We should try to make sure that a nondisclosure agreement has been signed by both parties before disclosing or receiving any proprietary information.

5. Any information we suspect has been obtained improperly or any non-public information contained in a competitor's bid to any government agency should not be used.

6. Any material we have reason to think may violate these standards or that may give the appearance of impropriety should be discussed with and turned over to the Legal Department.

7. A competitor's employees can't be used as sources of nonpublic information, either. Our new employees should not divulge proprietary information about their former employers, and we shouldn't ask them to.

8. Proprietary information about customers, suppliers, or partners shouldn't be used for inappropriate purposes. Nor should the information be inappropriately provided to other companies. We must make sure consultants and outside contractors are aware of and follow these guidelines. If you have questions about whether

the information is proprietary, talk to your supervisor or the Legal Department.

Carolyn:	Will—This is not a bad start. However, first, it needs to conform to your company's nomenclature—Egbertz does not use the term "legal department," but rather "legal team" (Number 6 and Number 8). Also, Monica wants the process called strategic intelligence, so that would have to be changed (Number 1) as would the associated definition.
Will:	Got it.
Carolyn:	Question: Does the company do or plan to do that much in government bidding? I had the impression that it did not do any, so most or all of point Number 5 should probably be deleted.
Will:	You are right—we do not do any and the incoming CEO has not signaled a change in that. I will delete it.
Carolyn:	Further, is misrepresentation of who you work for the only unethical thing the company should be worried about? By that I mean point Number 3. Maybe this issue should be carried over to the final ethical standards which will be redrafted in the future.
	Now, for Number 4—is the nondisclosure agreement suggested or should it be required? Make that clear.
	Finally, Number 8 is sort of vague. What is "inappropriate"? Can't the company use its own proprietary information or proprietary information it legitimately possesses for developing its own strategic intelligence? The way this is written, that could be an issue.
	So, if you can redraft this, and deal with these, I think you have a working "interim ethical policy." As with the other interim documents, make sure your successors know that they have to jump on these once they arrive.

Job Description

After discussing this, we decided that the existing CI team should help draft the job description for several reasons. First, Will, the current head of the CI team, had worked in this position at the former parent, so he was familiar with how that team operated strategically. Second, we are here to facilitate and walk them through the process, and not replace them.

Early Warning and War Games Brief

The same is true for the issue of early warning—should we just walk them through early warning? The question then arose whether or not the client would be considering war games as a tool? The title is unfortunate, but it is very commonly used, so we have to live with it.

We knew from our experience that discussing war gaming is best when it is a part of the early warning discussion. In fact, it can often be one of the most effective way of communicating the work and findings of the strategic intelligence team, including early warnings, to senior management.

What new problems did we run into with the client and how did we solve them?

Job Description

We sent Will an outline we developed to help him get started on drafting a job description. It identifies the differences between the skills needed for strategic intelligence collectors and those for strategic intelligence analysts.

Intelligence Skill Sets

Strategic Intelligence Team Skill Sets

For Strategic Intelligence Collectors	For Strategic Intelligence Analysts
Quickly identify and master relevant primary and secondary sources, their reliability, and validity	Analyze creatively—be able to put yourself in someone else's place and analyze accordingly
Know how to access and manage both internal (i.e., networks) and external resources	Use both inductive and deductive reasoning
Recognize anomalies in data and work around them	Have overview of basic analytical models and the ability to apply them
Continuously develop and refine research skills	Know when to use advanced analytical tools such as psychological profiling and patent mapping
Understand when and how to apply elicitation interviewing techniques	Recognize and deal with inevitable presence of intelligence gaps and blind spots, both personal and of data sources
Know when to stop collecting data	Know when to stop analyzing data
Adhere to ethics and policies associated with data gathering	Develop and deliver actionable analyses and recommendations

We let Will know that there were other issues to consider. For example, how many analysts are there to be versus collectors on the new team? While everyone probably needs some of these skills so that they can do both data collection and analysis, people should know which their principal responsibilities are when they join the firm.

The new CEO, Monica, had taken away the sterile argument that any new intelligence staffer must be knee-deep in the industry first, and, to a lesser degree, experienced in intelligence, second. She does not think much of the intelligence staff at her competitors, so Egbertz can start fresh.

From our other internal interviews, it was clear that the client is looking for a team of generalists, so it should get people who have a variety of strengths, and then assign duties as their unique strengths and weaknesses emerge. The client is not looking to hire one pure analyst and two pure collectors, for example.

We planned to remind Will to let the human resources people know that intelligence experience is to be favored over industry experience when they are doing their preliminary screening. That is how it should be in most cases. There are exceptions, like some aspects of the pharmaceutical industry, where there are unique intelligence issues and tools. But, in general, experience shows that you want intelligence experience over industry experience.

We also agreed to make sure that Will and human resources understand that, where they need analytical skills, it is hard, if not impossible, to train someone from scratch to analyze well. You can give a person the tools, but he or she still must have the skill, or at least some analytical skill, to start with. In other words, an analyst is born, not made. The issue is only how much training the client can give them once it has selected the candidates.

Early Warning

We were hesitant about dealing in depth with "early warning" for a brand-new team that was not yet in place. As we mentioned, and it bears repeating, early warning is more talked about than actually done—well. It requires patience, a lot of it, on the part of management because it has such a long-time horizon. We agreed to recommend that the client should look at this as a potential future role for the Intelligence team, but not as an immediate high priority task.

Our advice was that getting into that at this early stage will really complicate things for Monica. She sees one role for the new team and seems to be adding early warning only as an afterthought. While early warning can be useful, we agreed to suggest that the intelligence unit be positioned to grow into this.

A compromise would be to have the rebuilt team start with a shorter time horizon, say 1–2 years, for its early warning targeting. The client could do that by adding to the mission statement language to the effect that the team is tasked to "help identify the long-term trends that will drive the business and its environment." That way the client keeps its focus strategic, but the team is directed to think beyond one fiscal quarter or one fiscal year from the start of its work for the client.

For Monica, we wanted her to have something to mull over. Given all the changes, just providing an oral briefing will be one more thing for her to deal with—and forget—with as she moves up and her workload changes and grows. On the other hand, a written briefing stays with her. Also, with it, the new intelligence team has an idea of what she is looking at in an early warning program and what she expects as its deliverables when it is finally in operation.

Also, this way Will, the current head of the intelligence team, and human resources can have something tangible when they interview potential new team members. As for the team candidates, it really helps when you are starting a new job to know what new programs you will be expected to deliver and when.

What we generated will be an outline of the issues in creating and operating an early warning system. What the client has to do is to determine what she and the rest of her team want the new people to do once they are hired. In fact, they may have to experiment to work this out.

John drafted a long memo on this, which Carolyn then reviewed.

Carolyn: Woof! That is way, way too long for Monica. She needs only a high-level view. I would give her the first two sections only. The chart—may be yes, but the balance of it is way too academic. Then, the entire document can be used by the new strategic intelligence team when they arrive. They will need to be walked through it. Oh, change "CI" to strategic intelligence in the final version and get rid of the EWS acronym—remember, Monica does not like them.

Here is what John redrafted for Monica:

Issues in Early Warning

> **MEMO: Executive Issues in Creating and Operating Early Warning Systems**
>
> 1. Overview
>   A simple way to look at early warning systems is to consider the potential sources of early warnings events or trends. There are three such

potential environments—your firm's internal environment, its competitive environment, and its macro environment. In the chart below, we have added examples of typical early warning targets. As can be seen, only two of them deal with competitive and/or strategic intelligence. The third, the internal environment, should be monitored by the firm's own internal controls and processes.

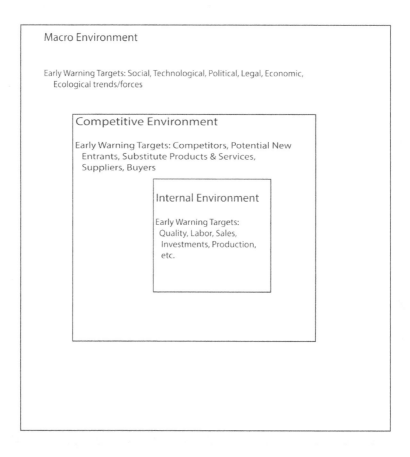

2. Intelligence Teams and Early Warning Systems

   If your intelligence team is to provide an "early" warning, then by definition, it must necessarily provide something beyond its existing current warnings. But before going further, ask yourself, do you **really** need an early warning system? If so, how big or broad an early warning system is best for Egbertz?

Consider the following questions to help you answer that:

a. Determining Your Need for an Early Warning System

	The Question You Must Answer	Your Answer	Impact on Your Need for an Early Warning System
Internal Factors	Do we need to quickly respond to competitive changes?	Yes	Lessens or eliminates the need
		No	Increases the need, as your firm needs time to prepare and implement responses
	What amount of resources do we have for the strategic actions?	Relatively abundant	Lessens the need, as, in some cases, money can be traded for time in responding to change
		Relatively scarce	Increases the need, as your firm needs more time to identify alternatives that would use fewer resources
External Factors	What kind of market cycles does your firm face?	Quick or short cycles	Long-term early warning system less useful; threats or opportunities can dissipate as almost quickly as they arise
		Slow or long cycles	Long-term early warning system more useful; changes will impact your firm for a longer time
	How concentrated is your industry?	Highly concentrated	Less, as each firm has some ability to control or impact the market's direction
		Highly competitive	Greater need, as each firm has less ability to control or impact the market's direction

(continued)

The Question You Must Answer	Your Answer	Impact on Your Need for an Early Warning System
What is the level of uncertainty in external competitive and/or macro environments?	Low	Less need
	High	Greater need

b. Scope of an Early Warning System

	The Question You Must Answer	Your Answer	Impact on Your Need for Early Warning System
Internal Factors	How dependent is your firm on outsourcing?	Low	Smaller
		High	Larger, as the fate of each source has a greater impact on your firm
	What kind of internal information sharing culture does your firm have?	Low	Larger, as your firm must have a greater focus on external sources
		High	Lesser, as a greater focus on internal intelligence networks can produce more critical data
External Factors	What is the firm's relative market share?	Low	Focus the early warning system more on the macro environment
		High	Focus the early warning system more on the competitive environment
	How complex is the business environment?	Simple	Smaller impact

(*continued*)

The Question You Must Answer	Your Answer	Impact on Your Need for Early Warning System
	Very complex	Larger need, and need to be dealing with more business units
How interconnected is your firm with other industries and regions?	Limited	Focus early warning system on local market/ industry
	Substantial	Focus early warning system on global market and on substitutes
What is the maturity level of your industry?	Relatively immature	Focus early warning system more on the macro environment
	Very mature	Focus early warning system more on the competitive environment

Carolyn: This is still somewhat technical, but at least it is a lot shorter. What do you have for the new strategic Intelligence team?

John: This, in addition to Monica's memo. That will serve as an introduction for the new team.

MEMO: Intelligence Team Issues in Creating and Operating Early Warning Systems

1. Types of Early Warning Systems

There is not just one kind of early warning system involving those in competitive or strategic intelligence. Rather, there are two separate kinds of early warning systems that an intelligence function might have to deal with.

i. Early warning systems for an internal customer

The first, and the one most people think of, is where an intelligence individual, team, or consultant (the intelligence function) provides long-range looks at the competitive environment and provides input to internal business customers, such as strategic planning, mergers and acquisitions, and long-range financial planning to support their decision making.

The issues here, exception for the filtering issues discussed below, do not differ much from anything else in the classic intelligence sense. That is, these are the same issues of clarity in the statement of needs from the internal customer, a focus on the getting necessary resources, and selecting research methodologies appropriate to the task, maintaining an ongoing data collection and analysis effort, and providing regular reports to the client. It is rare that there is need for an "alert" from the intelligence function to the end user during the early warning system process. Rather, the most effective and most common manner of communication is a regular briefing, whether oral, written, or both, to the end user.

The most useful early warning system to develop here is an early warning for your in-house strategic, rather than tactical, decision making. As we all know, any market can turn, and return, in a moment. Long-run trends are just that—long run.

ii. Early warning system for the intelligence function itself

The situation changes when the intelligence function seeks to create and use an early warning system for itself. Here, the intelligence function is in the unusual position of being both the end user or customer *and* the provider of the intelligence. That means, to do its work efficiently and effectively, the intelligence function must be particularly careful to focus on its own definition of the problem and on the structure and use of a kind of filtering process. Failure to do that will simply result in the intelligence function merely scanning the horizon, never looking for anything specific, and thus never finding anything of value.

iii. For both

The core issue here is, if we do not know what we are looking for and we do not know what is going to happen, how can we know what to look for and where to look for it. This is where the early warning system's management splits—in the first case, it is the end user or customer on whom the burden falls to define (or at least help to define) what is needed and to link the data needed to an action or decision. In the second case, the intelligence function must act as both client and analyst. And it must find a way to merge these two roles.

2. Phases in Developing the Early Warning System

A well-functioning early warning system process usually moves through several phases:

- Phase 1 is characterized by scanning to collect "weak signals," or to identify new trends and issues. The scanning itself relies primarily on examining a variety of media sources, plus accessing some primary resources, typically through wide-ranging interviews. This scanning activity is supplemented by reviewing previous monitoring of trends and/or issues by outsiders that have already drawn attention.

- Phase 2 is one of diagnosis that has two key steps:
  - In-depth analysis of the trend or issue, where the analyst is thinking creatively about how it could evolve; and
  - Examination of the various contexts of this trend or issue with the aim of gaining an impression of the *possible* potential development of an issue or trend, particularly trends or issues that may interact with each other.

  It is critical to select out the trends and issues that are most important to the firm. This is not only because the firm lacks infinite resources, but also because without this high-level filtering, all an early warning system can generate are indistinct, unfocused warnings, which provide little or no value to the firm.

- Phase 3 involves formulating a strategy to respond to the trends and issues that have been identified, labeled as relevant, and analyzed. When the intelligence unit is conducting the early warning for itself, the determination of the reaction/response is left to the appropriate end user on the intelligence team. It is usually up to the entire intelligence function to identify trends for which there can be a response. That is not the case when the early warning system is being run for one or more internal end users or customers. There the customer has to, or will, determine what actions are to be taken (or at least be recommended to others).

So, no matter how you describe it, the three-step process is to Scan, Interpret, and Act.

3. Figuring Out What You Need to Know When You Do Not Know What Will Happen in the Future

   The most overlooked practical element in making any early warning system effective is the necessity for filtering. Without filtering, you are looking at everything, without being able to draw conclusions. The proper use of filters helps overcome the following critical deficiencies and barriers faced when operating without them:

- Information overload.

- Failure to see what is important among that which is not.

- Inability to tie what is seen to the future of your firm.

The predecessors of today's early warning systems included within them some filtering, even if it was primitive or not even acknowledged. The most common such ancestors are the operations of lookouts on a ship at sea, or the operation of radar on an airplane in flight:

- Those who look to the analogy of ship's lookouts scanning the (environmental) horizon are missing the pre-existence of filters. Here the lookouts were not looking for everything everywhere; they were usually looking at the horizon or only a portion of it (which fixed the warning's lead time) and were looking for specific things, such as birds, smoke, ship's masts, mountain peaks, and ice bergs that warned of upcoming land or marine perils and opportunities. Even in wartime, a maritime lookout was scanning a fixed area for a limited number of targets for a limited amount of time. When the lookouts could not adjust for the optical changes in the areas that they are scanning, that is, adjusting their own filtering, they ran the danger of missing warning signs until the threats were quite literally on top of them.

• The "radar" analogy does not support skipping filtering either. Remember that radar is already pre-tuned, so that it picks some things and skips others, that is, it has a built-in filter. Otherwise, a navigator looking at radar in flight would simply see a screen filled with numerous blips, some moving, some not. By looking for everything, he would see nothing.

To build an effective early warning system, whether it is for the intelligence unit itself to broaden and deepen the products and analysis it provides for the firm or it is to provide actionable input on a regular basis to another corporate function, an early issue that has to be dealt with is the question of time.

No intelligence function will ever have enough time to process all the data that can possibly be collected. So, it must find a way to narrow what it is looking at. That is the role of filtering to narrow the amount of data to be monitored.

There are many approaches to using filtering to narrow the focus of the early warning program:

I. Start with your strategic plan and your intelligence KITs, if any. Then identify and analyze the assumptions they include about the macro and/or competitive environment, as well as assumptions about threats and opportunities facing the firm. For example, if one of the threats that has been identified, or which can be discerned during the strategic planning process, is the future availability of substitute products or services, then the data needed for early warning system might be the following, driven by the underlying assumptions:

  • Technological changes—the development of new or innovative production methods
  • Changes in the economy—changes that could impact the costs of substitutes as well as the purchasing decisions made by consumers and intermediaries
  • Political and legal changes—for example, in the pharmaceutical industry, new global trade agreements impacting the importation of drugs, or environmental and regulatory proposals that would make the *cost* of generic substitutes more expensive to produce in the United States. Also, that may include a focus on changes in the value of the U.S. dollar in the global market, which could change the cost of potential substitutes

II. Another quick way to narrow your scope, at least in the beginning, is to look at what events or developments came as "shocks" to your firm and/or its closest competitors in the recent past. Then try to determine what would have been the key indicators of these shocks at one, two, and three years out from them. Use them as a filter. Going out further than three years almost always makes this process unmanageable.

III. To narrow the focus, at least with respect to the competitive environment's early warning system, watch out for anomalies. You can often spot them because they are commonly associated with one of more of the following kinds of language:
- The presence of superlatives like *biggest, slowest, fastest, highest, lowest,* and *greatest*
- Descriptions of less/more such as *shortage, lean, pinch, rapid,* and *expansion*
- Reports of unprecedented growth or shrinkage
- Firsts, that is, events that are black swans or represent other disruptions
- Evidence of deception by your targets, such as disinformation, lies, and the presence of frequent denials
- Unintended comments, such as Freudian slips or gaffes (as when someone tells the truth by accident)

IV. An alternative for strategic early warning filtering is to look for things that "did not happen." By that, we mean relationships with suppliers, customers, competitors, or sources of actual or potential substitutes that might have occurred, but did not. For example, in one project we worked on, a firm in the health industry was offered the chance to join a venture to finance and eventually acquire technologies that might aid it and other firms similarly situated. This firm did not do so. Several years later, that same firm acquired a small information technology firm to expand its current services to its customers. Shortly after that, the (spurned) venture funded its acquisition of a similar firm. That acquisition undercut the value of the first firm's investment. Further intelligence research and analysis indicated that, preceding the acquisition, the venture had provided a large amount of funding for another information technology firm which then "led" the final acquisition. If the firm had tracked the venture's investments for a period of two to three years, it might well have seen this competitive threat emerging in time to take protective action.

V. Another approach is to create or define a set of "leading indicators," that is, events or actions that, in the past, have tended to be precursors to dramatic changes. As with other suggestions dealing with early warning systems, this is most applicable to early warning that the intelligence function provides about the competitive environment for its internal customers.

VI. Next come the data collection requirements. Here, management issues begin to diverge. Is the early warning system supposed to focus on specific competitors, including potential competitors (the competitive environment), or will it look further at the broader political and economic environment (the macro environment)?
- If the former, then the next step is to identify what activities by competitors or potential competitors would indicate potential activities that would change the direction and force of these firms. For example, would the acquisition of a new company with unusual research and development capabilities be something worth looking at because it might be a precursor toward changes in a competitor's product costs?
- In the case of an early warning system aimed at macro environment, the issues broaden much more quickly. The intelligence process then should no longer be focused on individual competitors, but rather should focus on industry, country, and even global trends that may drive strategic changes.

4. Other Management Issues

When focusing on data collection, the intelligence function must keep in mind the timeline, that is, how far in advance is it seeking to provide an estimate of possible activities or scenarios? One suggestion is to work backward in time from an actual past event that would have been important to the customers of the early warning system, to events that might immediately precede the targeted event, then to those events that would precede those, and preceding those.

Realistically, as you go back in time, you may appear to see that, in hindsight, virtually anything that became a shock was predictable. The reality is that it was never completely predictable; it was only one of many potential events until it finally happened. Before that point, any one of 100 items, events, or outside/inside smaller shocks could have changed the likelihood and eventually the occurrence of the one key shock. That means looking at and analyzing a bewildering number and variety of indicators. Realistically, you will never do that. That is why filtering is so critical.

Effective filtering may impact or even change the future. How? By enabling you to spot a coming trend in time to respond, you (and your firm) not only reduce the number of potential futures that can follow the warning sign but also may actually prevent or soften a significant shock.

How is that possible? Visualize a World War II freighter at sea with a lookout on duty. In a choppy sea, the lookout suddenly catches a glimpse of what might be a stick upright in the ocean. Even as it vanishes, he warns the captain of the possible danger of a nearby enemy submarine, which prompts the ship to undertake evasive action and call for an escort to attack the sub. Here, the presence of an observer changed a critical future characteristic of the event being observed.

We gave the first document to Monica and had the second held for the new strategic intelligence team. It was to be given to the members on their arrival.

What happened at the client after we were done? How successful were we?

We then doubled back with Monica for a short briefing on the overall work and on early warning issues, in particular. Later that same day, we met with Will to make sure that he had completed everything he needed for the search for new employees, that is, the interim job descriptions, mission statement, and ethical standards. Then, we then set a follow-up appointment with Monica to meet the new strategic intelligence team when it was in place. We went over all the documents, including the full paper on early warning systems, with the new team.

The new intelligence team, in turn, immediately went to work with the now-in-place new legal team to fine-tune all the interim internal documents and policies, and, at the same time, to bring the legal team into the intelligence loop. As it turned out, there was very little additional work needed by us on these documents.

At their request, we provided the new intelligence team with a short memo on producing an effective compliance policy and program:

Compliance with Policies on CI

While Egbertz's intelligence team is involved with developing a written policy on competitive intelligence the intelligence team must also deal with compliance with that and other programs. What does that include?

- First, compliance requires knowledge. That, in turn, means the intelligence team and any DIYers should be trained on appropriate legal and ethical issues, and that the training should be renewed on a regular basis.
- Second, all these people should always discuss specific ethical concerns with a supervisor. DIYers should be allowed, or even encouraged, to contact a designated trained member of the legal team with any legal concerns they may have.
- Third, make sure that all contractors, consultants, and other third parties whose services you use have their own formal, written policy dealing with the collection of CI data. You should review their current policy before any contract is signed or work begun on a long-term contract. Then, the contractor must be made aware of Egbertz's own policies, and agree, in writing, to be bound by them as well. If the firm's policies and contractor's policies are in conflict, then the better solution is to have the contractor bound by the stricter of the two policies.

- Fourth, every one of these firms should also agree that any CI work by its subcontractors will be subject to the same standards. Requiring that you (or someone from legal) review all such subcontracts is a good way to protect Egbertz, particularly from blind subcontracting. (Blind subcontracting is the handoff of an assignment to a third party without the firm knowing of the event. In some cases, the subcontractor may not know of the identity of the consultant's client.) Blind subcontracting is a quick path to chaos and problems.
- Fifth, if necessary, every one of these firms should be encouraged, or even required, to participate in company-approved training on legal and ethical CI issues.

At Monica's request, we then scheduled some training on early warning issues, as she had decided that the new strategic intelligence team should at least test the waters in this area. As an executive who believes in a long-range look at the market, she felt early warning of some sort was critical. What needed refinement was what could be produced and of how much value would it be to the client.

Monica also asked for some suggestions the new intelligence team could offer to the DIYers. Here is what we sent her:

Suggestions for DIYers

1. Aggressively seek out the data that you need, if you think you need it to complete your analysis. Who is to say that you are wrong? If you got that data, and found it did not help, next time you will do even better and be more efficient.
2. Network, network, network. 80 percent or more of what you need is probably in the hands or the minds of your associates somewhere at Egbertz. The best way to access it is to use you own network. You DO have a network, don't you? If not, create it. Then continue to nurture that network.
3. Have confidence in your own analysis and develop confidence in your judgments based on that analysis. If you do not have confidence, who else will? If you have confidence, others will see that and respond.
4. Be politely assertive, and do not be afraid of being wrong in your analyses. Everyone is wrong sometimes.
5. When you are wrong, acknowledge it, figure out why you were wrong, internalize that, and move on. That is called growth and maturity.
6. Don't be afraid of being right. If you are afraid of that, why are you still working here?

7. They—the competition—are not you, and never will be. Avoid mirror imaging your competitors at any cost. Mirror imaging is when you assume that your competitors are just like you, that they see things the way that you do, and that they will always act the way you would act. That is one of the greatest and most common traps in intelligence analysis.

8. Do not keep your key findings to yourself. CI is most valuable when it reaches—and helps—more people.

9. If everyone agrees with all your findings, then there could be something wrong. Have all of you looked at the situation with the same institutional blinders? Perhaps.

10. Don't take your CI work too seriously, or let your CI work take you over. Yes, it is useful, and even interesting, but you also have a life. Enjoy that life. Unlike intelligence personnel in government, your work will not prevent (or hasten) the end of times.

LOOKING BACK ONE YEAR LATER

Monica quickly set up the new intelligence unit, authorized it to establish a permanent mission statement, and immediately initiated training. She then assigned the team the task of creating an early warning system. That was all done within two months.

After the training, some six months later, the market had changed. As Monica anticipated, two of Egbertz's competitors left the market, almost at the same moment. At the same time, several of the remaining U.S. firms began cautious efforts to create some joint research and development mechanism.

Through the new strategic intelligence program, including its emerging early warning program, Egbertz had been watching for warning signs of such changes and was thus prepared for the sudden, radical changes in the market. In fact, it had positioned itself to be able to move so quickly that it picked up many customers set adrift by the sudden departure of the two firms before other competitors could react.

Nine months after the end of the assignment, the early warning reported that the former parent, Koatin, was probably going to be entering a cost-cutting phase. The team's assessment was that Koatin would try to reduce the costs associated with at least one of the two contracts it had with Egbertz.

Egbertz quickly began a confidential, internal assessment of the value of these contracts and concluded that only one of the supply contracts would be profitable in the long run. The other was going to be marginal in terms of profitability and probably could not be made very profitable. Egbertz then moved proactively, opening renewal negotiations with Koatin. As expected, Koatin pushed for the reduction of price in the soon-to-expire supply contract. Egbertz agreed to the reduction that Koatin sought, in exchange for Koatin renewing the second contract under its current terms for an additional five years. That preserved the profitable contract, while Egbertz also obtained the option of terminating the less profitable contract after 18 months.

So, in its first year, the new intelligence team, using its very new early warning system, had provided this valuable actionable intelligence, cementing its credibility with the CEO and with senior management.

5

Defending against Your Competitors' Intelligence Activities

THE CASE

About the Company

Anders Manufacturing Company is a medium-sized manufacturer, headquartered in the Mid-West. It has a factory and one warehouse there. It also has two factories and three warehouses in two other adjacent mid-western states, enabling it to serve a nine-state area with its warehouse direct shipping and maintenance. The sales force is composed of independent sales representatives, who also sell other lines of industrial equipment for other firms; some also sell products of competitors, but only in geographic areas not now served by Anders.

Its Management, Owners, and Employees

Family-owned since its founding in 1978, Anders Manufacturing is now run by Maxwell, the president. Maxwell is 54. Maxwell is the son of the founder, Byron. Byron died in 2000, when Maxwell took over. Maxwell's daughter, Rion, 34, is being groomed to join Anders and to eventually succeed Maxwell. She graduated with an MBA about eight years ago and is currently a senior manager for a major component supplier of Anders.

As a family-owned firm, Anders is very supportive of the local community and is always present at places such as farmer's markets, community festivals, and other local events. Maxwell says that this has been a "good way to try out new concepts and products as well as to support local activities." He sees it as a very creative way to combine marketing with support for the community in which his employees live.

A Look at Its Competitive Environment and Market Profile

Maxwell: Anders' sales have been growing slowly since recovering from a 15 percent decline during the 2008 recession. We currently have eight U.S. competitors. Six of them are independent, family-owned businesses, and two are subsidiaries of large U.S. equipment firms. Seven of these firms, as well as Anders, sell only on a regional basis; one sells only on a state-wide basis, in California only.

Because these products do not "travel well," our sales are limited to the area to which we can distribute directly. Also, these products require our, I mean the companies', support at installation. Any needed repairs are also supplied by the manufacturers. The nine firms in this business do overlap somewhat geographically, but none are nation-wide—yet. So, that means each of the nine companies competes with no more than two other companies in the areas that it now serves.

John: Is there one firm that causes problems for you?

Maxwell: Is there a problem firm? Yes. That would be the California-based firm, Frinng. Frinng is a subsidiary of a large German industrial group. It entered the market in 2014 on the West Coast, actually in California only. The German parent company has recently announced that Frinng will be selling on a "national basis," whatever that means, but with no dates or other details. We think that is because of possible product changes. You see, Frinng previously announced that its German parent is developing products for it that will "travel well," so that it can eventually serve customers across the U.S. But that is still in the future, or at least we hope it is. For now, Frinng's in-house sales force is operating only in California, but recently it hired an outside sales force which will be starting up selling in both Oregon and Washington states, I think. So, it looks like it is starting to expand its reach.

What were its plans? What is coming next?

Anders has been focusing on rebuilding its sales from the 2008 low. It is now focusing on expanding sales to existing customers, while researching product improvements that might enable it to compete more aggressively on a price basis. It has no current plans to expand beyond the region it now serves. However, Maxwell is planning to look at that option during the planning cycle later this year. For that reason, it now sees all nine firms as current or at least potential future competitors.

Status of Intelligence Operations

Anders has no formal CI activities. The information on the German parent of Frinng's plans came from an announcement in an industry publication that the marketing manager read and brought to Maxwell's attention.

Maxwell meets with his marketing and sales teams every week. He told us that Anders' independent sales representatives all file regular call reports on their sales efforts, which the sales manager reviews before each meeting. It is from these sales reports that Anders found out what Frinng is doing and where it is expanding.

After additional questions, Maxwell told us that the independent sales agents serving it also serve four of its other competitors, but none of these competitors now sell into Anders' "space"; the remaining competitors, except Frinng, have in-house sales forces. Frinng now uses a mix of both in-house and contact sales agents.

What problems/issues were identified by the client?

Maxwell: For everything we do, some other company seems to know it almost immediately. It's just as if everything we do here is being "followed" by one company and what they do in response then "spreads" to others very quickly. My prime suspect is the California-based firm, Frinng. As I said, Frinng is a subsidiary of a large German industrial group. It entered the market in 2014 on the West Coast. Although its parent company has announced that Frinng will soon be selling on a "national basis," they are not doing that now. However, they look like they are already mimicking Anders almost instantly on most changes we make.

What I do not understand is how Frinng knows what we are doing and, more importantly, what we plan to do. Because we are regional in our sales, we do not compete head-to-head with Frinng. Anders does not attend national conventions; we stay with regional and state exhibitions in our sales area. So Frinng is not present at these events where we are present. We have looked at our employees carefully and do not believe we have any one per-son who is spreading our business plans around the industry. This is a family business and most of our key employees have been here for years. They are all very loyal.

Right now, we are not losing sales to Frinng, but we are to some of the other competitors who mimic Frinng. My concern is that, if Frinng really goes national, when they come into our territory, they will be real trouble. And, of course, if we go national, we will be head-to-head with them almost at once.

The real issue, at least as seen by Anders, was defending itself against the CI activities of its competitors, or at least those of one specific competitor, Frinng.

OUR PERSPECTIVES

Key CI Diagnostic Quiz Results

How is Anders' CI team staffed, trained, and managed?

Anders' CI activities are informal, conducted by its president, calling on his sales force and other managers.

Yes

Anders' informal CI team has current industry knowledge.

No

Anders' informal CI team has no specific training on CI and has no experience in developing and providing CI.

How does Anders' informal CI team get its direction on targets, on its data collection, and on deliverables?

Anders' CI activities are informal, conducted by its president and other managers.

No

Anders' informal CI team has no clearly understood objectives or consciously identified the target audience it aims to serve.

Anders' informal CI team does not produce intelligence reports and assessments on its competitors and/or emerging threats they believe are most important.

Where does Anders' informal CI team get its data?

Anders' CI activities are informal, conducted by its president and other managers.

Yes

Anders' informal CI team uses primary/human sources of intelligence only.

Maybe/Perhaps

Anders' informal CI team uses both internal and external networks for its data gathering.

Anders' informal CI team sometimes uses secondary sources of information (public materials, analysts' reports, etc.) to learn about key competitors and/or new products and technology.

No

Anders' employees do not report information about our competitors or relevant emerging threats and opportunities to the appropriate managers.

Anders' informal CI team has no legal and ethical guidelines covering the gathering, use, and communication of CI.

What intelligence does Anders' informal CI team provide?

Anders' CI activities are informal, conducted by its president and other managers.

No

Anders' informal CI team does not prepare profiles of its competitors, including their business plans and strategies, or analyze its competitors' business plans and strategies to predict and anticipate their future actions.

What does Anders do to help its CI process?

Anders' CI activities are informal, conducted by its president and other managers.

Yes

Anders recognizes CI as a legitimate and necessary activity in today's marketplace.

No

Anders does not have a formal set of legal and ethical guidelines designed specifically for CI.

Anders' employees are not aware of its CI activities and how to contribute to and/or benefit from that activity.

What do Anders' managers and executives expect from and get from the informal CI team?

Anders' CI activities are informal, conducted by its president and other managers.

Yes

There is regular two-way communication between the informal CI team and senior management.

Maybe/Perhaps

Anders' management is willing to hear things that they might not want to hear from the informal CI team.

What results has the CI process achieved at Anders?

Anders' CI activities are informal, conducted by its president and other managers.

Yes

CI directly affects decision making at the senior level at Anders.

What were the real problems there? Why are they different from what the company said they were?

Defending against CI Activities

From our experience, we knew that we would have to dig deeper in this case before starting the client on a full-blown defensive CI program. What we have to do first is to get the client involved. Otherwise the client may see it, erroneously, as a once-and-done situation. That is, its team members ask the question, and we give an answer that solves the current intelligence leak, and that is all. That does not keep it from happening again in the future. If it happened once, it almost certainly will happen again.

Education on the Basics of a Defensive Program

In our conversations with Maxwell, we found him to be a very hands-on person. Based on that, we considered offering him a very high-level program to rapidly educate him and other key Anders' executives on the basics of defending against CI activities directed against them. Then, we can get the client to start into the defensive process without a major commitment at the beginning. With our parallel research on where their competitors may now be getting critical data on Anders, and after they are familiar with that is going on in their firm, we can help them move toward a custom, ongoing defensive CI program.

Where and how did we solve the client's real problems and help the client?

The two issues, defending against the CI activities of competitors and educating management on the basics of that, quickly merged into a single two-step process.

The first requirement was that Maxwell get all his key executives together for us. He said that was not an issue. However, looking ahead, the question of his daughter quickly arose. As the "heir apparent," to quote Maxwell, increasing Anders' sensitivity about the CI activities of competitors, and then launching a defensive program, if needed, should be something she knows about, and hopefully would buy into.

However, Rion, Maxwell's daughter, was currently working for a key supplier. Maxwell felt that her involvement at an early stage is critical, but was not ready to talk with her about the "copycat" behavior of one competing firm. She would be taking over from Maxwell, at a date he had not discussed with us or her, but Maxwell had to take over from his father while in his mid-30s, a similar age, due to his father's unexpected death. Maxwell had hinted that, due to his family health history, Rion could be joining the firm "sooner rather than later."

In addition, suppliers can be a potential source of CI to their own clients as well as a source of competitively sensitive data (which we call CSD) to others in the industry, potentially including competitors. For that reason, we wanted to get Rion involved early. So, we decided to raise this directly with Maxwell. But that final decision would be up to Maxwell.

If he was unwilling or unable to involve Rion now, then he could bring her in when Anders expanded its defensive program to cover suppliers and other third parties. We brought this to Maxwell's attention; he decided to bring Rion in when we started, but on a personal, not corporate basis, to avoid offending his key employees and managers. That sort of relationship in a family is a very sensitive one and it is usually best to defer to the wishes of the members of the family, and work around them to the extent necessary.

We told him that our first educational targets should be his marketing and sales teams. Maxwell had said that they meet with them every week, and indicated a while ago that they should be involved, so he quickly agreed.

He asked whether or not the outside sales representatives should also be brought in at the same time. We advised him that the outside sales representatives should come in separately—and later—since they are independent contractors. We stressed that they should not be a part of the diagnosis of the problem of anyone leaking or transferring CSD, at least at this point, but they should definitely be a part of any ongoing solution. Maxwell agreed, so we moved on.

Educating Management on Competitively Sensitive Data

As Maxwell requested, we kept the first round very short. Here is how it went:

> **John:** Maxwell, thanks for the invitation today. I want to talk with you and your team about the issues surrounding protecting Anders against competitive intelligence activities of your competitors. I am going to be very general, and I would like to get questions from you as we go.
>
> My presentation today is just 11 overheads, which I have already handed out to you. I also left a copy which can be uploaded by Anders for training future employees.
>
> Please ask questions at any time. I am here to work with you, not lecture at you.

What Is Competitively Sensitive Data (CSD)?

- CSD includes data from which a third party can reconstruct your trade secrets or other valuable competitive information.
- Most CSD is data that, if accessed by your competitors, would diminish your competitive advantage and/or improve theirs.
  - It varies from firm to firm.
  - Typically, it includes customer lists, product formulations, pricing tactics, total sales and profits, or sales incentive programs.

First, what is competitively sensitive data, or what I will call CSD? First, it is not a trade secret. A trade secret is a very different thing. Does anyone know what that means?

Answer: Something that we label or mark as a trade secret?

John: Yes, that is definitely a part of it. The whole concept of a trade secret is that it is something that has a value from being secret, and that you, the owner, must always treat it as a secret. That means if you fail to protect it, and it ends up in a competitor's hands, you have lost the ability to go to court to protect it.

However, if you can reverse engineer a trade secret from stuff that your competitor has put in the public domain, in your hands it is no longer a secret. Note that I said reverse engineer or assemble it. And that is what we are trying to keep a competitor from doing—assemble one of your trade secrets or other competitively sensitive data from the bits of data that you release.

Question: Isn't it a crime to steal a trade secret? If so, isn't doing what you said also a crime?

John: Good question. It is a crime to steal a trade secret. But, note I said **steal.** To the second question, the answer is no. If you can show you figured out a trade secret from stuff that is not a trade secret, that is, public, you are fine.

Simple First Steps for Dealing with CSD

- Your firm can do it even though it is not involved with developing competitive intelligence (CI).
- It is something that should be firm-wide.
- It is designed to protect against or foil your competitors' actual or potential CI activities.
- There are only a few simple steps for you to follow.

John: Now, what kinds of things do you men and women consider as CSD, competitively sensitive data? Let's start with Maxwell.

Step 1

- Identify which of your data are *truly* competitively sensitive.
  - Do not overprotect.

Maxwell: Well, the kinds of things that our competitors seem to find out about, which I think should be confidential, or as you say CSD, are our price lists, our repair success rate, our average response times, and our sales commission program. Also, since this is a private business, I think that our profits and gross sales are as well.

John: OK, that is a good place to start. Let me turn to the marketing team. Is the head of marketing here? OK, good. Of the data that Maxwell identified, that is, price lists, repair success rate, response time, sales commissions, profits, and gross sales, which of these do you know? I expect it would be the price lists, repair successes, and commissions. Right?

Marketing director: All of the ones you mentioned.

John: That's all of them? What about sales—is the sales director here?

Sales director: Here. We also know the response time in addition to the other three.

John: So, does anyone here other than Maxwell know the company's gross sales and profits? Hands? I do not see any.

　　　Are there any other suggestions for data that could be CSD? Remember, if your competitor knows it, it would be something that works to their advantage and/or your disadvantage.

Answer: New product launch plans.

Another: Names of the largest customers. And what about shipping costs?

John: Maxwell, do you see any of these three—product launches, customer names, and shipping costs—as CSD?

Maxwell: The first, new products, for certain. As for customer names, maybe just the newest ones. The largest buyers of our products —well, all our regional competitors already target all of them. Shipping costs—everyone faces them from the same carriers— we do not get any special rates, so I do not think that is an issue.

Step 2

- Assess your current CSD inventory's exposure.
  - Check your business's Internet sites as well as your social media sites, such as postings on YouTube and Facebook, for CSD already in plain sight. Take them down at once.
- Check employee sites for similar leaks and alert them to take immediate action.

John: OK, so now we agree on a preliminary set of CSD for Anders. This is not final. You can and should review this list regularly. Let me go online now to YouTube. On the screen, you can see here is a list of the YouTube videos Anders has already posted which are available right now. From what I can see, they are endorsements—the "we are very happy with your products and services" sort of thing. Are they useful?

Answer: Yes, they give our customers a feeling that we have great products—and that Anders is a supportive partner.

John: Now, let's look at these by date. There are three that were posted in the last 12 months. Are these from existing customers or long-established ones?

Answer: Two of the three are very new customers.

John: And the video gives the company name and first name of the endorser. Maybe there should be a cooling off period before posting new customers? Or perhaps a little less information online for a short time?

Maxwell: We can start doing that right now. We have two new customers, small, but growing. Let's protect that data.

John: Let's look at something else. Let's try Facebook. Here is one individual, self-identified as an outside sales representative of yours. Note that he is bragging about an incentive bonus from you. He must be very good. But look at the details in his boasting. Now, before you get upset, is there anything in his contract that bars this? Sales manager?

Sales manager: No. But there sure will be tomorrow (laugh).

Step 3

- Know where the company produces and stores CSD, who has access to it (including third party contractors), and review why they have that access.
  - A particular focus here is your system of independent distributors.
  - Never finger-point—you are just being thorough.

John: Let's go back to our working list of CSDs: new product details, newest customers, gross sales and profits, repair response times, price lists, repair successes, and sales commissions. What departments, outside of those represented here, know these or have access to them? Also, what about outsiders—suppliers, sales agents, distributors? Which of those know them or have access to them—authorized access that is?

Again, we are not in the business of pointing fingers or assessing blame. We are just trying to look at these things and see how it is that competitors seem to know what Anders is up to—and how—if that is possible—can we stop that. But, we cannot stop it if we cannot figure out where it might be coming from.

Question: How do we find it? Just ask them what they know?

John: No, not that way. What you must try to do is what your competitors may be doing to locate CSD on Anders to develop CI. Just as a first suggestion, run a Google search with your company name and each of these items and see what you can come up with. If you get a lot of noise, that is, hundreds of irrelevant hits, narrow the search to locate things like Word and PDF documents only. You may be surprised what you find. I already found an Anders price list, dated 18 months ago, which evidently was posted on your website, but otherwise hidden. By that, I mean it is not linked to your public website, but still has been located by a Google search.

I am going to guess that someone in sales put it up so that the sales team, and maybe your outside independent agents, could access while at a regional trade show. Does that sound right? Yes? This is an example of a perfectly appropriate action which can also accidently expose CSD. One solution is to take these down after their use is past. Or have whoever maintains the website routinely check for such postings and take them down after, say, 90 days.

Speaking of a trade show, has this ever happened? Someone walks up to your booth and starts to ask questions just a little different from what you expect. But they zipped past their name and affiliation very quickly. In fact, you did not really have time to figure out who they were. That can tip you off to an effort to start an elicitation interview.

And here is a war story to illustrate what I mean. Several years ago, Helicon was tracking the expected rollout of a new consumer product from a client's competitor. One of the ways we worked this was to call the toll-free service number for the target's consumer help center. I told them I was calling about this product—true—which I knew was available already in Atlanta—true. I asked when it might be available where I was, which was outside of Philadelphia—also true. The response was that the operator was not sure. I just remained silent. That silence prompted the operator to say, "Let me check with someone else for you on that." I thanked the operator and waited. The operator came back and said "I checked with my supervisor and she says in about four months." I replied "Yes?," nothing more. Again, the silence was filled by the operator: "Yes it will be rolling out nationally in three months and reach you by the fourth month. I hope you enjoy it." I thanked her. She was very helpful, after all.

Question: Why do you keep mentioning your silence? Is that important?

John: Yes, I am glad you noticed the mention of the use of silence. It is a very effective elicitation technique. People do not like silence in a conversation, particularly if it may be their "fault." In the customer service environment, in particular, everyone wants to help, and a caller's silence is often interpreted as a failure to provide help.

Now comes the underlying question: why was this CSD even available to the operator? It evidently was not immediately at hand, but it was available to the onsite supervisor, who, trying to help someone helping a potential customer, did what they are all trained to do—go a step further to help.

Step 4

- Work with third parties who have access to your CSD to sensitize them to the need to protect it.
  - Here, we are talking about your outside sales reps.
  - Make sure your agreements with them cover this point.
  - And, regularly remind them of their obligations—nicely.

And, getting back to your sales agents, make sure your agreements with them and with all, and I repeat all, third parties require them to protect your confidential information. And that ties into the next overhead. Some of your agreements probably already deal with protecting your trade secrets. So, work with legal and corporate security to get that protection language extended to confidential information, your own CSD.

Question: Is that all?

John: No. You should ask your contractors to remind their employees, who are after all indirectly working for you, that they are obligated to protect your confidential information. Maybe ask them to remind them once a year. What you are trying to prevent is having them sitting around at a trade show or in a bar and swapping stories about you that contain your CSD. And you know and I know that this happens. You cannot prevent it all, but you can make people sufficiently sensitive to it so that they are a little more careful.

Also, a lot of CSD slip out due to carelessness. Let me give you another true story. A client of ours, a product manager, was flying back from a trade show and went to her assigned airplane seat. Her flight neighbor already was working on his computer. She turned to talk with him and saw on his screen a big title, you know 44-point type, mentioning her product!

She looked odd and made a small noise. Her neighbor, taking her sound as initiating conversation, I guess, introduced himself as the product manager of a competing product. She muttered "I don't believe it." He took that as a reason to keep talking—to impress her, I suspect.

He then said he was working on a presentation on how to gain an edge on his own competition—her product. (laughter) I swear this is true.

Again, she said, "I don't believe it." Then, she said "That is wrong!" Her seat mate was visibly upset and challenged her with "What?" She said again "It's not right." He snapped "How the **** do you know that?" Her abrupt response: "Because that is my product!" (laughter)

Now stop for a minute. He was really stupid, very careless. He was revealing his firm's CSD. But what about her? She just told him that all his work was wrong. Who was more careless?

Step 5

- Work with your corporate security staff.
  - Reinforce protections against accidental release of CSD.
  - They already do that for trade secrets.
- Use simple tools like labeling documents as confidential, proprietary, and trade secret (if appropriate); avoiding computer and telephone work in very public spaces; and never using jump drives (which can easily be lost).

John: This is something that Maxwell and you senior managers have to work out. Remember, the goal is to protect the company, and not to punish anyone. So, if someone gets fooled into revealing something, it is better to know it, protect against that kind of leak in the future, and then move on. That way access to that CSD and perhaps other CSD is now closed off.

In any case, when you know that this sort of CSD has been compromised, you can try to deal with it.

Step 6

- Make sure your employees and third parties know whom to notify if they suspect the possible leak or loss of any CSD.
- This is not an enforcement issue, but an awareness issue.
  - Do not punish them—they are helping you protect other CSD.
- Very good CI collectors can collect a lot of CSD without your knowledge or cooperation—if you cannot stop it, you can at least make it a little more difficult!

John: Finally, just be calm. While CSD is, by its very term, competitively sensitive, the loss of one piece is not likely to be catastrophic. Of course, that is not the case with a trade secret, which is why they are treated differently. Also, don't lock everything down out of an abundance of caution—or paranoia.

Step 7

- Do not over react!
- CSD usually loses its value over time.
  - Do not try and protect everything from everyone forever.
  - If you do, you will be unable to do any business.

Question: How long should we try and protect them, I mean CSD?

John: That depends. For a new customer's identity, maybe six months. Does that seem right Maxwell?

Maxwell: Yes. By that time, our competitors will have figured out we captured that account and will already be bird-dogging it. What about a new product launch? How long would you suggest for that?

John: Once it is out, do you really need to tell your people to be careful? You probably want them to make a lot of noise, right?

Maxwell: I see what you mean. Only protect these CSD as long as they are still sensitive? Is that the standard?

John: Absolutely. Maxwell, I suggest that you and your team have plenty to work with to get started. I think that you should get the word out, review what you have posted on the Internet, and what has been posted by Anders on the "net," then talk to your contractors and employees, and continually keep your eyes open. If, after say four to six months, you still think that your competitors are getting the jump on you because they know what Anders is doing or will be doing, it is time to drill down further.

We can help you by reviewing what they could collect on you and the firm and trying to figure out if they, in fact, got inside information, or just conducted effective competitive intelligence activities against you. If necessary, we can help you develop a more comprehensive defensive program. But first, let's see if we have solved the problem the simplest way.

What new problems did we run into with the client and how did we solve them?

We agreed with Maxwell to follow up with him in six to eight months, after he and his team had worked with the very basic program we outlined for them. We privately suggested that Maxwell also bring his daughter, Rion, in on this, or at least brief her on it. As he said, she will eventually be in charge, potentially returning in a very short time. Also, we suggested that, while she is still working at a major supplier, maybe she can spot some leakages of CSD from Anders on her own—but not by spying on her employer—rather looking at the market from a different perspective.

We also left Maxwell with checklists and guides for his employees who would now be attending more trade shows, conferences, and meetings, to alert them to improving their operations there while keeping an eye on off-site security. Maxwell said he will distribute them to the appropriate staff for their review and education:

FIRST STEPS IN "WORKING" A TRADESHOW OR CONFERENCE

By tradeshow, we also include any conferences you attend that are attended by your competitors or other companies of interest.

The first thing you have to establish is to answer the question: why are you even going to this tradeshow? If you are going there solely to represent your company, and expect to be anchored to its table or booth or stand, then you have limited opportunities to develop any CI. However, even anchored there, you should be prepared to listen carefully to what customers and potential customers of yours may say to you during their visit to your booth. In fact, if you can really engage them in conversations, try—very gently—to elicit from them what they may have heard from one or more competitors at the show.

A better option, if you can, is to dedicate some of your time to visiting competitor booths, attending open sessions of the tradeshow at which competitors may be speakers or panel participants, and talking to people as they leave competitors' exhibits.

The ideal is that your preparation for this should include a commitment from the Anders that you will be doing this as your primary—preferably sole—mission. It is not an effective way to operate to get a commitment that "if we can spare you" you can then do some CI work. At a trade show, there is very little spare time.

What you should prepare for is a day (or even days) of listening, note taking (you can get an app for your smart phone to help you in dictating these on the spot), and a lot of movement. One definite "to do" is to dress *not* to stand out. By this, I mean if you are wearing a shirt or hat or button at your booth identifying you with your company or your product, lose it when you are working the floor, collecting competitive information. Alerting a competitor that your firm is now listening to one of its salesperson's pitches or studying a new product on display makes it almost impossible to collect useful data. If that means you have to bring in an extra shirt with you and change when you leave the Anders' booth, do it.

Notice, we did not say pretend to be someone else, use false trade show ID, etc. Legal and ethical is still the rule, as with all your other efforts to collect data for CI.

Regardless of what you are doing, regularly collect and then quickly preserve your impressions and information. Do this as you are going along if possible. If that is not possible, take time before you return to the office to record, either by dictation or in writing, all your impressions and data collected, including an evaluation of any and all materials that you have collected while at the meeting. By the time you get back to your office, not only will there be other, pressing, demands on your time, but also you will inevitably and quickly begin to forget individual details that might have been critical had you remembered them.

PREPARING FOR A TRADE SHOW

Before you work a trade show, consider these tips:

- Do not be afraid or nervous. What is the worst that can happen? Someone won't talk with you? Forget about it. Move on.
- Do interviews to supplement your pre-show secondary (desk, book, and Internet) research. Use these interviews at the show for things you cannot get otherwise, for updating older data, and for figuring out what will happen, not just confirming what has happened.
- What do you want to find out? Can you state it in one short sentence? Then say it out loud. Does it make sense? If it does not, change it. Never read it from notes or memorize it. People will spot that immediately and not talk with you.

- Allow enough time. Even though you think it will take only 15 minutes, always allow more. Maybe you will get lucky and the subject will be chatty. Do not turn off a faucet before it turns off naturally.

- Make sure you will not be interrupted immediately afterward so you can make good notes as soon as you are done.

- Be professional, and polite. Smile while you are talking. It really works.

- Watch your language. You will be surprised, perhaps even shocked, how much a "please" or "thanks" can get you. Even if a subject does not want to talk, ask, politely, if there is someone else that could help you and if you can use the subject's name. Regardless, of what is said, always "thank" the subject.

- Be patient. Maybe this is not a good time for the subject. If so, reschedule—right then—very politely. If the subject is discussing something that is particularly useful, keep it moving, using little nudges, like "really?" and even dead silence. Silence can be very effective. It may make the subject slightly uncomfortable, maybe enough to encourage him or her to add something more.

- Wind it up. When you have what you want, try to take the conversation quickly to something else, so that the final impression left in the subject's mind is not the critical data you were seeking, but that something else. Then, again, "thanks."

- When you are done, end it, and then go and dictate your notes. Then write up your notes into a full document as soon as you can. Never put either off. You will forget something, maybe small (to you) comments, maybe an inflection that could be important later.

MORE THOUGHTS ON WORKING TRADE SHOWS

One of the most productive ways to produce your own CI is to learn how to work a trade show, expo, or conference. What should you be doing to check out your competition at a trade show? First we will touch on what not to do: do not pretend to be something or someone you are not. In most trade shows, you will have a badge identifying you by name and organization, probably color-coded as well to indicate whether you are a vendor, a potential customer, the media, an outside attendee, etc. Honesty is the best policy. Be who you are. Do not fly a false flag.

Now, once you are there, you should immediately look at the registered list of vendors and determine which of your competitors are actually present and, perhaps as importantly, which ones are not present. Did you expect to see particular firm there? Why are they not there? That may mark the beginning of an inquiry into a potential new opening in the market space when you return to the office.

Now take a quick look at the floor plan. Who spent a lot of money on space and who seems to be spending less money than last year or vice versa? Those

buying more space or more expensive space than last may be more dangerous to you in the near term than they are now, or at least they may think they
will be. The reverse could be true for those that cut back on marketing
expenses at the trade show. Does that change in spending mark something
significant to you?

Do not be afraid to walk around and look at your competitors' displays or
even to take a picture from outside of the booth. It is an open session and
you are behaving openly. If you are working with a team of several people
at the trade show, it would be useful to detail one or more of them to actually
visit the booths, displays, etc., to listen to what your competitors are saying,
and to see what they are displaying.

One thing you must be sensitive to when planning to work a trade show is
that your competitors might be, in fact should be, working there against
you. What can you do about that?

In theory, you could bar them from entering your area. But that really is not
feasible if you have a very large exhibit. If you have a small one, and you
see someone of them hanging around, you could politely ask them to leave.
If they don't, frankly there is nothing more you can do about it, except to note
whose employees were doing this.

What else you can do is to look at your exhibit area. Of course, it was set up
to attract customers by showing them new and different things by emphasiz-
ing new features of products, etc. But by doing that are you giving away vital
information to competitors? Your approach should not be to deny your competitors access to all information. That is pointless and impossible as well.
Also, in trying to do that, you going to deprive your customers and potential
customers of information as well, cutting into sales. What you must do is
determine what is competitively sensitive, at least for short time, and work
to keep that, or at least some of that, away from competitors. Arrange your
exhibit space to do that. For example, keep detailed brochures on new products in the back, managed by an employee who records who gets a copy.

Make sure that your people will realize that their job is to talk to potential customers, actual customers, the press, etc., but not to competitors. At a trade
show, there is no such thing as a safe conversation with a competitor. Give this
message directly to your salespeople. In many industries, it is common for the
sales staff to concentrate on "qualified leads." That is all well and good, but to
some salespeople, this means that any person who is not immediately seen as
a qualified lead is to be handed off, however gently, to someone else, very often
a technical person. This is not a very good idea. Why?

From personal experience, we can tell you that the technical staff are more
than happy to talk about your product, in fact to brag about it. The problem
is they could be talking to the wrong person. In addition, since they are often
add-ons to the tradeshow staff, they feel somewhat neglected and easily
respond to elicitation techniques.

Once you hit the floor at the meeting, what do you do?

- First, take care of your own business, the reason you and your firm are there. Never desert your booth or exhibit space to check on your competitors unless you have someone else, a qualified person, covering it.
- Second, think out your approach. What is it you are trying to find out?
  - Is it the presence of new competitors? If so, carefully go over the show catalog and plan to work the aisles where new competitors might be housed, particularly if the show is organized by type of product or service.
  - If your concern is new potential competitors, allow more time. Review the ads in the show catalog. Do any of these seem like they are attacking your niche? Are these companies located in an area at the meeting where they have not been in the past? If so, do they deserve some initial attention because of that?
- Third, are there some of your key suppliers at the show? If so, you should visit them to keep the lines of communication open. Also, that is a great time to find out from them if they have been contacted by any of your competitors. It does not help you if one of your key suppliers suddenly switches allegiance from you to a competitor, or is talking too much to one about you and your products or services.
- Fourth, if your concern is new products from existing competitors, then you are going to have to focus on going to the exhibits of each of your existing competitors and making careful notes of what is going on. When you go there, if you can, take pictures. Do not be shy. You are not doing anything improper. If they ask you to stop, do so.
- Fifth, if you can, you, or another member of your team, should circulate through the venue at the opening of the first day, so that you can pick up copies of all merchandising, product, and capabilities materials at every key stand. Remember, the longer you wait, the more likely it is that something that could be critically important to you will no longer be there for you to get and read.

CHECKLIST FOR SECURING OFF-SITE MEETINGS

There are simple steps that should be taken at your off-site meetings to prevent the accidental release or purposeful capture of sensitive or confidential information, whether to competitors, the media, or the public:

1. Find out who else will be holding meetings the same time at the site you are considering using. While you may secure your site, when your people are taking a coffee break, they start talking in the hall and others may overhear their conversations. You should do this at two points: first when you're considering retaining this site, and second, just before you go there to see if things have changed.

2. Make sure you check-in everyone that comes into the room. Outsiders can wander in "accidently."

3. If you are going to have a registration table and/or display table, consider putting it inside the room or rooms you'll be using rather than the hall. If you place it in the hall, then you need to have somebody of the table all the time to keep the materials secured as well as to keep prying eyes (and hands) from things like attendance lists, notations of incoming calls, etc.

4. If you are distributing materials at the meeting, distribute them at the meeting, not before. In fact, distribute them in the conference room, not in public halls of the hotel or convention center.

5. Clearly mark all materials as company confidential, proprietary, etc. This will not stop some people from taking these materials, but will discourage those who operate on an ethical basis. It will also alert your attendees to be careful with them.

6. Remind the people there that what you are doing at the meeting is confidential and is not to be discussed outside of the meeting rooms, including in the halls, at the bar, the pool, on the golf course, etc. No discussion outside of the room means *no*. In addition, remind them that any materials you hand out are to be handled with care. If it is a very sensitive matter, you may consider having people leave all such materials in the room and then locking it at the end of each day.

7. Keep communications in the room secure. Have all attendees turn off all smart phones and tablets. That is aimed at keeping attendees from recording the proceedings or taking pictures, as well as communicating with outsiders. If that is not possible, ask that these instruments be put in airplane mode, so that no incoming or outgoing calls can be made. This also cuts down on distractions for the presenters.

8. When you are done with the meeting, secure the room—yourself. Do not rely on the hotel staff for this. Securing means collecting all materials and notes left behind, wiping all whiteboards completely, and removing all conference materials from trash and recycling cans and taking it with you. Securing a room during the meeting sessions, but then leaving copies of the agenda with a whiteboard showing some conclusions reached on a new marketing campaign is not good security—it is folly.

What happened at the client after we were done? How successful were we?

Six months later, as promised, we contacted Maxwell. He discussed the work that Anders had been doing on a basic defensive awareness program over several months. He was pleased with its progress, although he had "not yet gotten to the reps (independent sales representatives) with it." As Maxwell said, "it is already going pretty well in the results." Anders found out a lot about how that competitor, Frinng, was getting the jump on them. It turned out to be a combination of factors.

The first part of it was no surprise, as in our experience, leakages of CSD often start at or close to the top. In Anders' case it was from the top and then all over. At least once Maxwell gave an extensive interview to a local business publication where he discussed some things about the company, including its income—in general terms, he said "roughly." But that article put some-thing about that CSD out there that its competitors could not generate on their own.

Also, the sales and marketing people all knew CSD was critical to selling, such as the repair data, new product launches planned, that sort of thing. And, of course, they used them, properly, to try and entice existing and potential customers. Some of that data eventually got to Frinng—from these customers and potential customers.

We asked Maxwell how Frinng found that. He said it was because Frinng told both its inside and outside sales representatives that it wanted to get such data. And a few of its outside sales rep firms overlapped with Anders' firms. Since no one at Anders told its outside reps or their firms that they were to protect Anders' CSD—its CSD moved on.

Carolyn also talked to Rion, Maxwell's daughter, who still worked at an Anders supplier. She said that "most of the stuff Maxwell is concerned about is already common knowledge" at the supplier level because "we know that the sales reps all talk with each other." She said that they, the sales reps, exchange information on commission schedules, since that is where the money is for them, as well as who is easiest to work with—that is, who gives you the most support for your pitches. And, the reps did not worry about this because "no one ever told them to be concerned." And while Anders is regional, the outside rep firms it uses overlap with those in other regions, so "they know each other, or know someone in common, etc."

Finally, Maxwell acknowledged that he has been forced to sit down and decide what is really CSD. He now understands that some of this must be made available widely to make sales and to service its customers. We think Rion may have helped open his eyes on this, but cannot be sure. Also, for-tunately he did not drift into paranoia—the "No one talks about the busi-ness without talking to me first" attitude, shutting down all outside communications. That is an occasional problem with business people suddenly confronted with the fact that their competitors know way too much about them.

Maxwell and Rion, as well as the senior staff, are now beginning to realize that there is a lot of intelligence out there that maybe, in Maxwell's words, Anders "should be digging for." Rion, who will succeed him, is a lot firmer. She thinks that Anders needs to "get really aggressive—and now" with respect to CI since "they are using it against us—so we should use it against

them." And, we learned that she will be returning to the firm as a senior offi-
cer in the next year and a half, probably as executive vice president, with
Maxwell serving as chairman for several years before she becomes president.
She indicated that Helicon will see "some more action from us" after that.

LOOKING BACK ONE YEAR LATER

Within nine months after the end of the assignment, and well before she
was expected to return to Anders to join Maxwell, Rion rejoined the firm.
The reason for this accelerated schedule was that Maxwell, her father,
became seriously ill. Unlike his father, Maxwell did not die suddenly, but
his health deteriorated quickly. Maxwell stepped down, with Rion replacing
him as president. Maxwell remained somewhat active, as chairman emeritus,
but limited his activities to chairing meetings of the board of directors.

Rion hit the ground running. Anders' competitors quickly tried to expand
and move into some of Anders' current territory following news of the transition. Foremost among them was Frinng. However, Maxwell has not imple-
mented a formal intelligence program, so these actions and their scope came
as a surprise.

Also, Maxwell's efforts to reach out to the independent sales represen-
tatives with training on protecting Anders' CSD were not yet completed.
Unfortunately, that meant that its competitors had more insight into
Anders' actions than Anders' had into their actions.

Rion was able to stabilize the situation quickly, but Anders lost about
10 percent of its overall sales. Faced with this situation, Rion reached out
to the suppliers to keep them loyal to Anders, and also to keep them from
becoming a source of information on Anders' situation. That was successful.
She then contacted the independent sales representatives to stress their obligations to protect Anders' competitively sensitive information.

As the sales situation stabilized, Rion reached out to Helicon and asked us
to return to help her set up a full-time CI process. "We can never be caught
like this again," she told us. Within two months, she had a full-time CI program up and running. Within three months after that, her program warned
of Frinng's coming move into Anders' territory. Anders moved aggressively
and protected its existing clients. It then launched its own counteropera-
tions, moving into Frinng's territories as a part of Anders' own expansion
plans. Frinng was caught completely by surprise.

6

Adding Strategic Intelligence to Market/ Tactical Intelligence and Contracting Out for Market/Tactical Intelligence

THE CASE

About the Company

Cortelyou Financial Services (CFS) is a second-tier player in the U.S. financial services industry. It has recently launched an initiative to expand in what it regards as "underserved and emerging" economies in Central America and Eastern Europe. It wishes to use this expansion to extend the reach of both of its major business units: investment banking and institutional product sales. It also has two smaller, minor units, which it will keep focused on the United States.

CFS, like many of its competitors, is often very short-term oriented. While it prepares annual budgets, historically it has periodically instituted spending freezes within specific business units of one to two quarters in length when it faces or fears facing a downward trending market for that unit's products. In other words, if CFS sees falling sales or believes that its two major units will face declines in sales, it acts to cut its expenses almost immediately.

Its Management, Owners, and Employees

Historically, senior management at CFS comes from the top performers in investment banking, sales, and institutional product development. The company tends not to recruit laterally for employees from outside of the firm, preferring to add to its own staff holders of graduate degrees in finance or economics degrees right out of graduate school. The schools from which it recruits exclusively are in the United States, the United Kingdom, France, and Germany. The executive partners, that is, those in charge of one of the business units, have been with CFS for most, if not all, of their careers.

A Look at Its Competitive Environment and Market Profile

CFS is facing U.S. markets where it sees its competition is increasingly consolidated. Also, it is wary of growing too large in the United States, as it views its long-term regulatory climate as one where "the larger the firm is, the greater the regulation it is subject to," as its chair has put it. Unlike its larger U.S. competitors, it is not yet labeled as "too big to fail," so it does not yet face the additional burdens that come with that designation. It believes that careful non-U.S. expansion will provide it with significant growth, while spreading the usual risks of doing business, all without triggering additional regulation in the United States.

What were its plans? What is coming next?

CFS expects the U.S. financial services market to grow more slowly in the next four plus years than some overseas markets will grow. So CFS is looking to expand its activities into some global emerging market countries during that time, those where it sees greater opportunity for growth. However, it knows that it currently lacks any way to monitor those markets or to assess actual and potential partners and/or competitors in these markets.

Status of Intelligence Operations

CFS' current CI activities are conducted by a team of four members, all of whom are located in the market research department. All of them started with CFS as market research specialists and transferred to CI when the CI team was created about three years ago. The market research team, totaling an additional nine people, is headed by a 20-year veteran market research specialist to whom the CI team also reports.

CFS' sales force relies heavily on the work of the market research department, including the CI team. However, some in the sales force also do some of their own independent market and competitive research "on the fly" because "we cannot wait since the market and our clients do not wait" as one sales person put it.

It appears that virtually all the CI being developed for CFS is tactical. It may be because of that CI does not report to senior management. An alternative thesis is that the CI team does not produce strategic intelligence *because* it does not report to senior management. In any case, there is no evidence that senior management regularly receives or even sees any work product from the CI team.

What problems/issues were identified by the client?

Senior management says that it now wants to have the existing CI team develop "early warning" intelligence for CFS, with its focus on the newly targeted non-U.S. markets. This would be in addition to having them continue to provide tactical CI for the sales force for the new markets.

OUR PERSPECTIVES

Key CI Diagnostic Quiz Results

How is CFS' CI team or individual staffed, trained, and managed?

Yes

CFS' CI team has a clear understanding of who their internal end users/ customers are.

No

CFS' CI team has no specific training on CI.

CFS' CI team has no process to train interested and appropriate personnel in the skills and tools necessary to collect primary information and to analyze and then disseminate information to appropriate end users.

How does CFS' CI team get its direction on targets, on its data collection, and on deliverables?

Yes

CFS' CI team focuses its tactical intelligence efforts on competitors and products/technologies that management has identified as important.

Some sales people provide some of their own CI.

No

CFS' CI team has no systematic process for identifying and defining its intelligence needs, given its clients' expression of their needs.

Where does CFS's CI team get its data?

Maybe/Perhaps

CFS' CI team probably uses secondary sources of information (public materials, analysts' reports, etc.) to learn about key competitors and/or new products and technology.

CFS' CI team may use primary/human sources of intelligence in addition to secondary sources.

No

CFS' CI team does not appear to have established a set of legal and ethical guidelines covering the gathering, use, and communication of CI.

What intelligence does CFS' CI team provide?

Yes

CFS' tactical intelligence program systematically collects, analyzes, and disseminates intelligence to those people in our firm responsible for market planning and decision making.

No

CFS' CI team does not analyze our competitors' strategies to predict and anticipate their future actions.

CFS' CI team does not provide significant trend analyses to determine potential new forces in the firm's business environment that other parts of the firm, focused on performing their daily functions, might not be aware of.

What does CFS do to help its CI process?

Yes

CFS recognizes CI as a legitimate and necessary activity in today's marketplace.

Maybe/Perhaps

CFS' sales force's use of CI may be measured in their regular performance reviews.

No

CFS does not ensure that its CI team members are provided professional education in the areas they are primarily responsible, such as data collection and analysis.

CFS does not provide education on ethics and legalities of CI to all employees involved in any intelligence activities, even to DIYers and others outside of the CI team.

What do CFS' managers and executives expect from and get from the CI team?

Yes

CFS' management supports its tactical intelligence activities and uses CI effectively in sales and marketing.

Maybe/Perhaps

There is regular two-way communication between the CI team and senior management.

CFS' management may be willing to hear things that they might not want to hear from the CI team.

No

CFS' business managers do require strategic CI inputs for key program reviews.

What results has the CI process achieved at CFS?

Maybe/Perhaps

CFS' CI team or individual may have identified measures by which it determines if its activity is effective.

CFS' management uses CI at some levels of decision making (i.e., tactical at present).

No

CFS cannot identify the past and current strategic impacts of the CI process, such as changes in management processes or in its strategies.

What were the real problems there? Why are they different from what the company said they were?

Need for Early Warning

CFS' professed need for early warning, having been expressed by individuals not now getting any CI, sets off a warning bell with us. It was an all too typical case of executives wanting something and applying what they consider to be the correct, or at least a "trendy," name to what they think they want. Before going further on this, we felt that we needed to talk in more depth with some of those partners who said that they wanted early warning intelligence.

Two executive partners in the firm, one heading investment banking, Martine, and one heading institutional products, Brett, talked with us about their needs and perceptions.

Martine: Currently, our sales group, actually sales groups, working for investment banking, have the market intelligence they need in the U.S. In both of our units, they are aggressive and successful because we are on top of, or even ahead of, our competitors. However, moving into Eastern Europe, we need a broader, 50,000-foot view of the market place and the current occupants.

Brett: Don't forget Central America; that is where we in institutional products are looking as well.

Martine: Sorry.

Carolyn: So is the expansion just banking in Europe and products in Central America?

Martine: Yes. We each hope to extend the other part of the firm there after the first group has a solid foothold, probably in two to three years.

Carolyn: Brett, what questions do you need answered by this new intelligence team that you cannot get answered right now? In other words, what decisions do you have to make that you cannot make now without intelligence?

Brett: Well, in the case of Central America, which non-U.S.-based firms have significant operations in our top five targeted countries? By significant, I mean with at least 10 percent of the market. We think that they could be good partners, or, failing that, dangerous competitors. I mean, they are already there, they know the market, they are local, and they have cleared all of the economic and cultural barriers.

John: So it is a threshold issue, right? Something you need done before you set foot there?

Brett: Yes.

John: What happens once you get there?

Brett: We will need help in tracking our competitors, profiling our potential customers, tracking regulatory changes and trends, that sort of thing. It is like hiking. We need a map, a guide, and a lookout depending whether we are camped or moving.

Carolyn: Martine, the same questions for you?

Martine: For the investment banking side, it is a little different. We are not looking to partner with a local firm. Ideally, we would like to purchase the investment banking business of an existing firm, one with the licensing, etc. already in place. We know that it is costly in the short term, but, in the long term, it means we can get going more quickly, with some established entrees.

Right now, we do not know who might be willing to be approached. In fact, we do not know all of the firms that have investment banking operations in these countries, much less if they are willing to consider selling the unit. So, we need help there.

Carolyn: And then . . .?

Martine: We would need help understanding any clients we may acquire, plus the ability to scout, actually support the scouting, for new business.

John: Do you see CFS starting in all four of your target European countries at once, or starting in one and expanding?

Martine: Ideally, I would like to get up and running in all four at once. Doing it the other way is significantly less appealing.

John: Does CFS have a cut-off scenario? That is, if events do not achieve certain benchmarks by dates certain, CFS will roll up some or all of these operations? Or is the commitment permanent?

Brett: Let me speak for Central America. If we cannot find the right partner or partners, we probably will not go forward. Building up the required local infrastructure, contacts, and regulatory approvals would probably be way too much for our business unit.

Martine: As for Eastern Europe, if we find the right acquisition, we will be there for the duration. I was trained in Germany and know that area fairly well. But, if there is no acquisition right now, we might hover—that is, wait and watch—for up to two years. Absent a good acquisition or even combination of several purchases in that time, I would recommend looking elsewhere. Of course, changes in market and political conditions in the EU and elsewhere in Europe could rapidly eliminate our interest.

Brett: The same is true in terms of politics and regulations in Central America.

Carolyn: As for the early warning intelligence you feel you need, how do you see the relationship between your business units and these individuals providing it?

Martine: I think that Brett would agree with me that, given the sensitivity of the intelligence and its connection with major firm investments, it would be best if these people reported directly to a senior person on the relevant team. Do you agree, Brett?

Brett: Absolutely, since this is very sensitive, high-level intelligence. The fewer people involved with it the better.

When we got back to the office, we both quickly agreed that CFS' executive partners' real needs varied substantially from their stated needs in several key ways. First and foremost, what they wanted was not an early warning system. Rather, it was, at best, an intelligence function that, either on an expanded or separate basis, could provide them with more strategic intelligence.

Second, from their interviews, it did not seem that they saw a reason for a strategic intelligence process past the establishment of their new operations in Central America and Eastern Europe.

Locating Strategic Intelligence Operations

Carolyn: Taking the issue of strategic intelligence first, its location within the firm could be a potential problem. The current CI team, which focused on market-level intelligence, is in the market research function, where it reports to a long-time market research manager and serves only with the sales and marketing staff.

That means that new strategic intelligence operations, if located where CI was already found, would be in what our experience indicated was in a poor environment. Our professional experience indicates that CI teams do not function as well as they might if reporting to or through, a market research team.

John: A large part of this is cultural: CI is in many ways a qualitative operation while market research is heavily quantitative. This difference is even more true with strategic intelligence.

Carolyn: The second issue that emerged when we carefully reviewed conversations with the two executive partners was that neither partner saw a role for this strategic operation beyond the expansion; whatever strategic intelligence CFS needed would be for the short term only.

John: I think that a solution to these problems would be for CFS to obtain the necessary strategic intelligence through contract services, that is, to hire two or more firms to provide the needed strategic intelligence—at least one for Eastern Europe and CFS' investment banking and at least one for Central America and CFS' institutional products.

Carolyn: I agree. These firms should then be direct reports to the business units that they support. But these firms should at least have regular meetings with the existing CI team, if that team would be supplying the market intelligence in the new areas once the expanded businesses were located there.

John: Neither partner had even considered this issue, but I feel, and I am sure that you do too, that this should be dealt with now rather than later. If tactical intelligence in Europe and Central America would be provided by local employees, then reporting through the existing CI unit and then through market research back to the local unit would probably not be needed.

Carolyn: But there is still one other, often major, problem. The markets into which CFS is seeking to expand, Central America and Eastern Europe, include nations where actionable CI is difficult to develop. Sometimes the data needed does not exist or cannot be accessed and/or the data's reliability cannot be assured. The client must be made aware of this and of the need to bring this issue up immediately when dealing with any potential outside contractors. That way both sides can be clear about what is possible, what is not, and what is expected to make sure they are all in sync before starting any work.

Staffing Non-U.S. CI Operations

Our decision to propose that CFS solve its temporary non-U.S. strategic intelligence needs by contracting out was based on several considerations:

- The two executive partners both appeared to view their need as transitory.
- The firm's budget history of hiring and then releasing workers could run into problems in parts of Europe. Some countries have very strict policies on

employee retention, making it costly and/or legally difficult to release employees there.

- Hiring and managing such people for a full-time position at a distance would tie up a considerable amount of CFS' time in the United States. On the other hand, using an appropriate intelligence firm, based in Europe, would provide the intelligence gathering capability together with local supervision.

The Rise and Control of DIYers

One additional issue that we spotted early on was the question of DIYers. Our first rounds of interviews indicated that many members of the sales forces were often doing some of their own CI research, evidently because they felt that the existing CI team and/or market research team were not fast enough in responding. Senior management approved having Helicon dig further into this.

Where and how did we solve the client's real problems and help the client?

Adding Strategic Intelligence Capabilities at a Distance

Using an intelligence firm based in the appropriate region—Eastern Europe and Central America—allows CFS to get local assistance in staffing up its regional CI needs. In fact, it may be a useful option for the client to continue to use a local firm if there is a chance that CFS might roll back these new operations within a few years. If the operations become permanent, then local staffing needed can be recruited for intelligence operations and hired to provide permanent support.

Merely saying that CFS should hire two firms—one for eastern Europe and one for Central America—to provide strategic intelligence for a limited time does not resolve its problem. There are at least two additional issues:

- finding the right firms;
- contracting with and managing these firms.

On finding an appropriate firm, the CI world is a relatively small one. Many established U.S. CI firms have non-U.S. contacts, formal or informal, that can provide some assistance in finding a local firm. The issues CFS will face here are the following:

Checklist for Screening Non-U.S. CI Provider

- Language(s). The client will need a firm that has employees who are fluent in English, to communicate clearly with. The firm also will have to be very fluent in the local language(s) its new operations will serve.

- Experience. Providing actionable CI can vary widely from country to country. In fact, the ability to conduct effective research will vary widely from country to country. So, any retained firm should have local CI experience. That could mean hiring more than one firm, as providing actionable CI in Poland will differ greatly from doing that in Bosnia.
- Ethical standards and local customs. CFS must establish a clear ethical and legal compliance program, insisting that its contractors adhere to its own standards. However, it must learn, from the contractors, what is and is not accepted locally. For example, while U.S. CI firms generally have no problem making calls to former employees of a target, in some European countries, that is frowned upon.
- Conflict of interest. This is can be troublesome. For example, CFS may find a CI firm for Central America, which is experienced and fits all other requirements. However, CFS must have a vetting process to assure that the same firm is not now, or has not recently been, working for a competitor. The problem is that CFS may not know at the beginning which competitors it will be targeting. That could mean conducting this review at least twice.

Having found the right firm(s), CFS must contract with it. Here, there are additional issues:

Checklist for Non-U.S. CI Provider Contract

- Future conflicts of interest. After the contract ends, since this is seen by CFS as a relatively short-term contract, will the CI firm be barred from taking on CFS' intelligence targets as clients? If so, for how long?
- Confidentiality. CFS must have a strong confidentiality clause in its contract. It may want to consider having the CI contractor return all materials it has provided back to CFS at the end of the contract.
- Local law. The local firm should identify any local laws, which may impact performing the contract, such as EU directives on privacy, which may impact collecting and retaining certain kinds of information on individuals.
- Term. The contract should have its term clearly spelled out, with provisions for either party to terminate it during the term with reasonable, say six months, notice.

We communicated these concerns to both executive partners. Following their review, we then sat down with the legal team to go over these in more detail so that the lawyers were prepared for the coming negotiations. The process then moved along smoothly.

DIYers

DIYers are not just an issue now. If there are changes in the operation of the existing CI team, for example, by adding work from Europe and Central America, CFS could see the rise of additional DIYers within the sales force who have come to rely on the CI team. They might feel that they cannot rely on the team for timely intelligence as the result of overloading the existing staff.

One problem with DIYers is that they generate their own "intelligence" without appropriate training to assure quality, without awareness of legal and ethical issues that could cause problems for CFS, and without having any way for the CI team, and thus others in the firm, to benefit from that work.

There are two options here:

- The first is to bar it, that is, tell the sales team that they cannot do their own CI research and analysis. Our experience shows that this approach rarely works. CI is already increasingly becoming ingrained in the jobs of many employees whose job description does not even use the word "intelligence." Also, those already doing it at CFS will resent this move, since their use of DIY techniques arose, at least in their minds, from inadequacies in the CI and market research teams' support and/or availability.

- The second is to manage and thereby harness it. That entails recognizing that DIYers exist, reaching out and training those who do it, or might do it, on basic techniques, as well as on the legal and ethical constraints on its collection and usage. That training is best done by the CI team, which has the expertise and experience. Also, by reaching out to the DIYers, the CI team begins a process of creating an internal intelligence network. Not only can the DIYers in the sales force provide the CI team with intelligence, finding out the areas in which they dig on their own should help the CI team better focus its own efforts. Also, once a good working relationship is established, the CI team can, and should, turn to the sales force for help in developing actionable intelligence for the balance of the sales team and for other internal customers.

We decided to discuss both options to CFS, but to caution them that the first was only given in the name of completeness. The Helicon Group could not recommend it under the circumstances.

What new problems did we run into with the client and how did we solve them?

Carolyn: This all uncovers yet another issue—based on my interviews with them, the CFS CI team is already understaffed and/or overtasked. The existence of some acknowledged DIY activity confirms that.

There is probably even more being done than is being acknowledged. Adding the responsibility of working with the DIYers to the CI team's existing workload would only generate more DIYers at the client. So, I have to disagree with your second option. We also should suggest to the client that the existing CI team needs expansion. Adding at least one more person would also allow the CI team to connect with the new (temporary) strategic intelligence contractors and the eventual (permanent) CI teams in Europe and Central America.

John: OK. But, there is another problem. CFS has traditionally hired from outside recent graduates. To add to the team, they are going to have to find recent MBAs who at least have had some courses on CI.

Carolyn: Is that hard? You are a member of the International Association for Intelligence Education (IAFIE)—what do you hear there?

John: It is hard, but not impossible. The number of universities offering CI courses has been increasing gradually, at least according to the members of IAFIE, all of whom have taught about some kind of intelligence, governmental, business, etc., at the university level. So, we should recommend to the client that, if they are not going to add someone to the team with on the job CI experience, they should at least add someone with some CI education—perhaps even from a private certificate program. There are several groups in the US and at least one in Europe that offer these. That kind of supplemental training might not be a bad idea for the entire team—not a full certificate program—that can be anywhere from 5 to 30 courses—but at least some additional formal training.

And that is what we recommended.

What happened at the client after we were done? How successful were we?

CFS retained several non-U.S.-based CI firms to help it in its expansion. Using our guidelines, the company quickly realized that it needed several firms in Europe, due to local language, legal, and cultural issues. Its results were mixed. CFS, despite our cautions about the differences and difficulties in conducting CI outside of the United States, expected that these contractors would provide CI at the same levels and of the same quality that its own CI team did. In a couple of cases, it was disappointed, but at least it was not surprised.

LOOKING BACK ONE YEAR LATER

As CFS went forward overseas, it developed CI capabilities in the new non-U.S. operations and added a member to the U.S. CI team to support them. As the non-U.S. operations grew, the executive partners found that they now wanted to get the kind of intelligence the new operations were getting, to feel comfortable with their ongoing development. These partners then transferred the CI team member responsible for dealing with the new operations to be a direct report to them. Within six months, they added some strategic intelligence responsibilities, that is, looking at the long-term issues, to supplement the CI work, looking at short-term, tactical issues, to this now two-person team.

However, a currency problem suddenly impacted its non-U.S. operations negatively. Some of its competitors had foreseen this and were prepared, but CFS was not. The problem arose before they began strategic intelligence operations. Despite the cautions given by Helicon, CFS then tried to reduce its non-U.S. CI capabilities by terminating employees, reverting to its short-term orientation. CFS quickly ran into problems with local laws and political pressure making layoffs difficult and costly. It was then in the position of still paying for some of these services, while receiving little for its payments. Similar personnel problems also arose when CFS tried to roll back other employment in the non-U.S. operations. In the United States, CFS transferred to the members of the intelligence team working with the non-U.S. intelligence team to other responsibilities.

Within three months after the currency problem, CFS put the Central American institutional products operations up for sale. The investment banking operations in Europe were stalled until the currency issues could be resolved, which was expected to happen within a year. CFS then expected to continue to expand the investment banking operations into the four target companies as planned. The CI operations had performed as hoped and smoothed the expansion.

7

Bringing CI Inside

THE CASE

About the Company

Numerosity Inc. is a private IT-based firm that focuses on the "Internet of Things" or IoT. Our secondary research indicates it is a midsized, non-public company that has grown both through organic growth, that is, by developing new products and bringing in new customers, and through several small acquisitions. The organic growth was largely in its first years, while Numerosity has made four rapid acquisitions over the past five years to continue to drive its growth. The result is that Numerosity has five operating strategic business units (SBUs): one is based on its original line of business and each of the other four is based on the subsequent acquisitions.

Its Management, Owners, and Employees

The firm is now in flux. The chief financial officer (CFO) position is being filled, temporarily, by its chief operating officer (COO), Vic. Its CEO is Margaret.

Margaret: Numerosity has recently successfully transitioned from management by its founders to a second-generation management team. Our senior management team is split about 50–50 between Numerosity employees who joined the firm in its early days and lateral hires made by Numerosity more recently.

We then looked at the next tier of employees. We found that the long-time Numerosity employees dominate in the central functions, such as planning, as well as in the R&D function. Lateral hires, that is, people who joined Numerosity from other companies, dominate the other traditional corporate staff positions. There were virtually none in the parent company from the acquisitions.

The COO added some detail to this:

> **Vic:**   To control headcount, Numerosity relies heavily on using contract employees and consultants. This is true not only at the corporate level—it is true in all of our strategic business units.

But the CEO, Margaret, then noted that "We have to minimize this outside contracting across the board."

A Look at Its Competitive Environment and Market Profile

A recent article on IoT reported:

"The buzz around the Internet of Things revolves around increased machine-to-machine communication. And that is built upon cloud computing and vast networks of data-gathering sensors in homes and businesses. The Internet of Things is based on 'mobile, virtual, and instantaneous connections.' Its advocates claim it will make everything from traffic lights to airports to home electric systems 'smart.' One source calculates there will be almost 60 billion devices on it by 2020."

Numerosity identified its current competitor firms as including a U.S. "unicorn," that is, a privately held start-up IT firm with a value of over $1 billion. Its other current competitors include government-owned firms in both Canada and France, as well as the subsidiaries of at least nine U.S. Fortune 1,000 firms. These all compete with at least one Numerosity subsidiary. None of these firms compete directly with all five of Numerosity's SBUs, but some currently compete with more than one.

The key parts of the global IoT market that Numerosity now focuses on include healthcare, industrial management, and government contracting.

What were its plans? What is coming next?

The IoT marketplace is a very fluid one and still somewhat undefined. Its scope is still developing, but there is a lot of attention being paid to it by both large and small companies.

Numerosity is currently trying to consolidate its growth as well as to make additional acquisitions.

Status of Intelligence Operations

The CI function at Numerosity reports to the CFO. Vic is only an acting CFO until they get a full-time CFO in place. Vic's primary job is as COO.

Numerosity, from our first round of interviews, appears to maintain a completely centralized CI function, which is consistent with the company's policy of centralizing other activities like market research.

At present, Numerosity has three full-time employees in the corporate-level CI unit. This CI unit serves both the strategic and the tactical intelligence needs of the parent company as well as all the SBUs.

All employees doing CI for Numerosity started their careers with Numerosity in either market research or in its sales operations. None of them have had any experience outside of Numerosity in CI or any specific outside training in CI.

Based on their backgrounds and the fact that they report to the CFO, it appears that the kind of intelligence the CI staff now delivers is heavily "numbers oriented." That is Numerosity shorthand for the delivery of heavily quantitative data rather than qualitative data: 3.6 percent growth rate in the third quarter versus intent to divest a subsidiary in the fourth quarter, that sort of thing.

What problems/issues were identified by the client?

Vic was the first we spoke with about their situation.

> **Vic:** We have a centralized intelligence unit. However, we are considering additional acquisitions, so this is a good time for us to look at the entire CI process. Frankly, our CI system was set up when we were a single company—now we are really just six related companies, or, more correctly a holding company with five operating strategic business units. Who knows? We may grow even further soon. What is the best way for us to proceed in CI while things are still this fluid?

Vic's background includes time with one of the top management consulting firms. In a later interview, he discussed the intelligence process a little more.

> **Vic:** At that firm [the consulting firm], I worked predominantly in strategy development and execution. So, I have a lot of experience with using competitive intelligence in strategic planning and financial planning as well. The reason I called you is that I am convinced that the CI process as it operates now is going to soon result in difficulty due to an increasing work load, and due to the additional work to be generated by future acquisitions. In fact, I am not sure that our own corporate CI team is up to the task of providing CI for us now.
>
> When will a new CFO be hired? Well, we are in the process of interviewing one now. I think that will happen in the next six weeks or so.

OUR PERSPECTIVES

Key CI Diagnostic Quiz Results

How is the corporate CI team staffed, trained, and managed?

Yes

The corporate CI team has experience in developing and providing CI.

The corporate CI team has a clear understanding of who their internal end users/customers are.

No

The corporate CI team has no specific training on CI.

How does the corporate CI team get its direction on targets, on its data collection, and on deliverables?

Maybe/Possibly

The CI team may produce intelligence reports and assessments on our competitors and/or emerging threats they believe are most important.

Business/program/product/technology managers are possibly responsible for providing some of their own CI.

Where does the corporate CI team get its data?

Maybe/Possibly

The corporate CI team probably uses secondary sources of information (public materials, analysts' reports, etc.) to learn about key competitors and/or new products and technology.

The corporate CI team may use primary/human sources of intelligence in addition to secondary sources.

No

The corporate CI team has not established a set of legal and ethical guidelines covering the gathering, use, and communication of CI.

What intelligence does the corporate CI team provide?

Yes

The corporate CI team prepares profiles of competitors, including their business plans and strategies.

Maybe/Possibly

The intelligence program probably systematically collects, analyzes, and disseminates intelligence to those people in our firm responsible for business planning and decision-making.

The CI team may analyze competitors' business plans and strategies to predict and anticipate their future actions.

No

The CI team does not see its mission as ambassadors of CI within the entire firm, using training as a communication vehicle.

What does the firm do to help its CI process?

Yes

The firm recognizes CI as a legitimate and necessary activity in today's marketplace.

No

The CI team does not ensure those employees involved in CI activities are given basic intelligence training.

The firm has no formal set of legal and ethical guidelines designed specifically for CI.

What do our managers and executives expect from and get from the corporate CI team?

Yes

The firm budgets both time and money to the CI process.

Maybe/Possibly

The firm's management is probably willing to hear things that they might not want to hear from the CI team or individual.

No

The CI program is run by a small group of people, who are not professionally trained to produce CI for the management unit's varying needs, including business planning and decision-making.

What results has the CI process achieved at the firm?

Yes

CI directly affects decision-making at the senior level in the firm.

Maybe/Possibly

The firm's CI activities often meet end user/customer needs on an ongoing basis.

No

Management does not use CI at all levels of decision-making (i.e., strategic, tactical, budget, planning, etc.).

What were the real problems there? Why are they different from what the company said they were?

Operation of Corporate Intelligence Team

One of the first things that we noticed was a potential cultural issue, one that could cause difficulty now and over time. None of the senior managers at

Numerosity seem to have come in, or rather up, from any of the existing acquisitions. It is not as if there have been no outsiders joining Numerosity. As we found, it has made lateral hires for some corporate functions in the parent company. But the absence of personnel from the acquired SBUs was evident.

Digging deeper, we were told that none of the founders of Numerosity are involved in senior management anymore. We confirmed that neither the founders of nor senior managers of any of the acquisitions are now involved in Numerosity's senior management. From that perspective, Numerosity looked like a very closed entity. Companies like this may not be open enough to new ideas or change, regardless of how dynamic and trendy their market-place may be.

Further research included interviews with the senior-level directors as well as to the operating heads of the SBUs. What we found was that Numerosity has tended to let its acquisitions operate relatively autonomously with respect to both R&D and product development. However, Numerosity has and still does retain "substantial, almost absolute, control" as one SBU executive put it, over sales and marketing, human resources, finances, market research, and, importantly for our work, CI.

Use of Outside CI Contractors

When we dug into the operational details of the CI unit, we talked to its director, Ken, who was not very cooperative at first. That changed as the assignment went on.

> **Ken:** The corporate CI team relies heavily on contacts that were made for them by the founders of Numerosity, that is, our "old boy/girl network." As other companies have joined Numerosity, we have continued to utilize the same process, that is, building up a network of contacts through the founders of each of the acquired companies. My Numerosity CI team regularly uses outside competitive intelligence research and analysis firms. In the past two years, we used three different outside firms to supplement our work.
>
> **Carolyn:** How much work do they do?
>
> **Ken:** Quite a lot, actually.
>
> **Carolyn:** Are any of these firms on retainers?
>
> **Ken:** I would prefer not to discuss that. I know you are working for us, but they are competitors of yours, aren't they? I need to talk with Vic about this first. I hope you do not mind.
>
> **Carolyn:** Of course not.

This interview raises more issues. While the company heavily uses contract employees now, the CEO, Margaret, had previously said that she has not used contract employees on a regular basis and wants to minimize Numerosity's use of such contractors and consultants across the board. So, we will have to dig into the outside contracting to figure out what help the CI unit will need in the future.

Where and how did we solve the client's real problems and help the client?

First-Stage Interviews

Before we could get into what is going wrong, we had to take a brief look at what is going right, or at least what the client *thinks* is going right. To do this, we worked our way through a brief diagnostic checklist when we talked with senior management, with the people that are using CI, and with those who are providing the CI. Here is the start of that checklist:

CI Diagnostic Checklist for Preliminary Interviews

Do you need CI? How can you tell?

> For a company or unit without a CI person or team, why do you think you do not need CI? To identify potential new threats—can CI help? What kinds of CI can help you?

> To identify recurring threats, internal and external—can CI help? What kinds?

Could CI have helped you in the past? Look at past avoidable recent failures in marketing, acquisition/divestitures, sales performance, product development, and unexpected competitor successes.

[For the CI customers] What do you expect CI to do for you? What do you do with the CI you get now?

[For the CI providers] Are you doing CI now? What kind? For whom? What do they do with it? How useful is it?

Are your competitors doing CI? How effectively? In other words, are you effectively flying blind?

These are necessarily open-ended questions. When we conduct interviews at the client, these are the major questions that we will start with. The lower level material provides prompts for our interviews.

After discussion, we decided that we should add to the interviewees at least one person from the outside CI firms that Numerosity now uses. By this time, we had found that Numerosity relies quite heavily on outside CI contractors and that the CI team uses four of them, not three, on a regular basis. That makes them a key part of the existing CI process.

So, we had to get the name of a contact at a CI firm from Ken as well as Ken's permission to talk with him or her. The firm's representative should not talk with us without Ken's consent, since such CI firms should be operating under a confidentiality agreement of some sort. Eventually, we asked for names from at least two of the firms. By talking with more than one, if we want to refer to something someone at one of the firms said that is critical or sensitive, it will not put their relationship with the client in jeopardy because we will withhold his or her identity.

We then reinterviewed Margaret, the CEO, Vic, the COO/CFO, and Jack, a vice president and the head of R&D at Numerosity. CI now reports to Vic and R&D, Jack's responsibility, is one of the CI team's major internal customers. Jack joined Numerosity eight years ago directly out of Stanford's graduate school. He worked at a major retailer for about five years before getting his MBA at Stanford.

While we interviewed them separately, of course, here is a combined look at what they both said.

Margaret: You ask how well does our CI team function. Well, they do not work directly for me. They work with research and development, sales, and marketing, and provide strategy for us and for our SBUs. By work, I mean they get assignments that support these groups, and deliver the intelligence directly to these internal customers.

What other teams are supported by the CI team? Well, anyone [in Numerosity or its SBUs] can contact them for help. Actually, they would have to contact the CFO first. You would have to ask the CI team who else they regularly assist—I do not know. The CI team reports to Vic, as CFO. They also provide him with CI to support strategy development in his position as COO.

As for performance, I have heard no complaints. As I recall, their budget has been growing due to increased demands from the growing SBUs. By growing I mean they are growing in number and in size.

Vic: Yes, the CI team reports to the CFO. Why? I don't really know why. They did that when I got here. Most of their work is done for the SBUs, particularly in sales and marketing as well as in the R&D [research & development] area. Well, to be more precise, much of the sales, marketing, and R&D are done at the corporate level. So, they also work, I guess, indirectly, for the SBUs. They provide me with background profiles of our major competitors, each fall as a part of the preparation for our annual planning cycle. Are they involved with the planning meetings? They have not been. No one has asked for that to happen so far.

Most of their work is done for the SBUs, as I said. Each SBU has its own needs.

Jack: I rely on the CI team during the planning process. I think that the competitive profiles they provide are very helpful. Financials? They are very good on the financials and on marketing numbers. Research & development? R&D is hard to track in this sector. People doing it do not always have titles that disclose that.

During the rest of the year? CI has a newsletter, biweekly I think, that they circulate and that covers industry developments, including R&D, stuff that is interesting. We [R&D] do not give them specific assignments about the competition. If I need something like that, I ask the sales force what they have heard, as well as talk to my [R&D] team about what they have read and seen at trade shows and conferences.

We later interviewed Tony, president of one of the subsidiaries of Numerosity. He was executive vice president at the subsidiary when Numerosity acquired it about four years ago. His background is in sales and marketing.

Tony: I deal with Ken [Manager of CI at Numerosity] when we are doing our annual planning. He provides me with profiles of our key competitors. Does he do them all internally? I do not think so. Some of them are clearly provided by outside firms, but they are all usually very good.

Other CI users in my SBU? Well, not really. A lot of the people who use the CI are managerial imbeds upstream [in Numerosity]. By that, I mean the research & development folks there, who do much of our R&D as well. Also, the marketing people get regular reports from them, which our people also see. Where do they get them? Our people get them from their corporate counterparts.

How impactful are they? Well, they all provide useful information, information that we feel we want to know about the competition. No, I cannot think of a decision I have made in the last year that was made or changed because of the CI I got.

The CI Newsletter

We first decided to deal with a small issue, but one that could be a symptom—the CI newsletter. We needed to get a recent sample of the newsletter that the CI team prepares and circulates. While any newsletter is always a low ROI—return on investment—product, we felt we should look at it because it was an established product.

Sometimes a client just does not want to get rid of it, even if it is not cost effective. And sometimes the CI team wants to keep doing it on the basis that everyone "expects" them to produce it. Also, to be frank, it is not a lot of work in some cases, so there is a "why bother" attitude when it comes to change. We both know of situations where the internal newsletter is produced on an outsourced, even overseas, basis.

Our experiences had led us to a mantra on this—If your internal clients see the newsletter as the CI team's main—or only—product, it is easy to think of CI as just a subscription service. And subscriptions are easily canceled.

When we asked for a copy of the newsletter, we also got a little more detail.

> **Ken:** I am sending you the February newsletter. It goes out about once a month now. I or one of the team members does it when we can get to it. This issue was very short. Right now all of the senior officers in Numerosity get it—around 8 people. Also, the CEO of each of the SBUs gets a copy. As for alerts, we do send them out as needed. There have not been very many in the past year or so.

Numerosity Market News
February 15

Canadian Government Exits IoT

The Canadian Government has finished its withdrawal of LeafNet from the US. This withdrawal began, without any formal announcement, about 3 ½ years ago. While Canadian Government officials declined to be interviewed about this, industry observers speculate that the decision reflects two factors: first, an increasing focus by the Government on developing businesses to serve the Canadian market as distinguished from global markets; and second, increasing costs of R&D in a government sponsored venture which were not offset with adding marketable products and services.

Source: *IoT Observer,* January 22 issue. Click here for access to this blog's full text.

In taking about this, we did not completely agree what do to about the newsletter:

> **John:** As you can see, the newsletter is not very good. Numerosity essentially just forwards materials from industry publications,

blogs, newsletters, that sort of thing, to its readers. I checked and confirmed that they do not include anything from the field sales force. Of course, that could be because the sales force is not in the CI loop. That has to change. The sales force can be a powerful resource for spotting emerging issues.

Personally, I am not happy with the use of the firm's logo. It makes the newsletter look like an announcement from human resources that they will be setting up enrollment for benefits online next week, that sort of thing.

Also, there is no punch to it. For example, why is **this** story important? I mean, Numerosity now has one less competitor in the U.S. Their caption shows no analysis of the story from the client's perspective, so the headline does not add any value. The CI team should at least rewrite the captions using our favorite trick: SWOT. That is, use one or more of the words—strength, weakness, opportunity, or threat—in the caption. Here, it could be "Canadian withdrawal from U.S. provides marketing opportunity," that sort of thing.

While they provide a link to the original article, that is so library-like. What is worse, there is no indication that this document was prepared by the CI team, no email link in the newsletter or extension number to allow contact for more information. It is just a one-time, one-way, throw away communication.

Carolyn: I agree with some of what you are saying. However, if you remove the corporate logo, it will diminish the limited impact of the newsletter even more. Without a strong name and logo, it starts to look like an even lower level communication of the "I will read it when I get to it, but it is not really critical to deal with" variety. Also, if it is so valuable, why didn't Ken know exactly to whom it goes off the top of his head? That makes it seem like the CI unit does not think it is worth their time.

If they are going to do this, they have to do it right—to get more out and get it out more often. Once a month is not a CI newsletter—it is a note from your grandmother. Look at the time between the blog posting and the distribution at Numerosity— 23 days. With this type of delay, people will not look forward to getting it—it just becomes one more thing to get out of the way without reading it because it is filling up your inbox.

And it needs a new title—"market news" is bland, and hopefully not accurate. It should be "actionable intelligence" or something along those lines. And then it should provide that, which this sample does not.

Look at this case. Numerosity's senior officers should have known about this sea change earlier. It goes back over three years. If they did know it before this newsletter, then this newsletter looks useless to them; if they did not know it, then that three-year failure is the CI unit's fault.

To be fair to the staff, putting out a newsletter weekly or even more frequently ties up personnel time—possibly excessively. Recall Ken's comment about doing it "when" they can do it. That does not seem like the CI unit sees it as a high priority.

With newsletters, you also have to make sure that people don't see the CI newsletter as just another ordinary company newsletter. You know, the kind that includes "Mary's birthday is Friday and there will be a cake in the solarium at 1:00 p.m. Everyone is invited. Try out for the company softball team." That kind of newsletter.

Assuming their officers actually read it—and Ken should have checked into that in the past, because our interviews did not indicate that they do—maybe the CI team could contract out the development of a regular focused release of secondary content. Then they can use their time and expertise to rewrite the captions in the SWOT style, to eliminate any story with cannot be captioned using SWOT, and to add a "field trends" section as the team develops with material from the sales force.

Also, they have to avoid using too many acronyms. "IoT" means, at least to most of the people at the client, the "Internet of Things." But it also stands for the "International Optical Fair Tokyo," a huge trade show, to others. Using too many acronyms does not add clarity—but it sure can engender confusion. What is even worse is that this acronym is not standard—some people in the industry use IofT instead of IoT.

If the CI unit finds that their internal audience does not use the newsletter, they should just send out critical as needed alerts and shut this down. But, if they keep doing this, they have to take clear ownership and use this to drive their internal customers back to them.

We decided on what to say, and to leave this for the final report. There, we will stress that this is their newsletter. The client must decide if it has value, and whether they want to upgrade it or just get rid of it. They cannot leave it in the current, useless, limbo.

What new problems did we run into with the client and how did we solve them?

As we dug deeper into the CI operations at Numerosity, we met again with Ken, the head of CI there. Ken had been with Numerosity for eight years, five years of that in sales. He has run the CI team for the last three years, which means he came in as the CI team's director, even though to us it did not look like he had any CI experience. We developed this information from Ken's LinkedIn profile as well as from the company's brief biographical information on its home page.

> **Ken:** How did I start in competitive intelligence? I was involved with sales at Numerosity for a while, and enjoyed it. I started digging into what my competitors were doing before I made calls, and drafted proposals and pitches. I found that there was stuff I could dig out that made us look better or made them look weaker, or both. So, using that, I did better. Then, when I became a manager, I started helping others in sales do the same thing. Then Jack [the head of R&D] heard a presentation I made at the sales planning retreat, which R&D [research & development] sponsored. It was letting us know what was in the competitors' pipeline, that sort of thing. He arranged for me to start doing that sort of work. I mean intelligence, for the R&D team.
>
> From there, the demand grew and I soon added two other employees. From where? Inside [Numerosity], of course. We run internal competitions for all new positions. One person was from what was then called financial operations and the other was number two, I think, in the strategic planning office.
>
> What training do we have? Well, the last to join the unit, the one employee who did planning, went to a CI session at the ASP [Association for Strategic Planning] annual meeting right after he joined the team. I have read several books on CI. The second team member and I listened to a couple of webcasts on intelligence. So, I guess you can say that we have learned on the job—but hey, that is the Numerosity way.

From there, we went after information on the outside CI contractors. As we discussed, John got permission from Ken to talk with contractors.

John then talked with one member of an outside CI firm, Curtis, the owner of CI4. CI4 is a private CI firm, with one full-time employee, Curtis. It also has several contract CI researchers. To put it more bluntly, they are freelancers whom CI4 regularly uses. CI4 has been working with Numerosity for more than five years. That means they predated Ken's time at Numerosity.

> **Curtis:** CI4? That stands for competitive intelligence, strategic intelligence, technology intelligence [CTI], and defensive intelligence. I have been a contractor with Numerosity for almost six years. I was hired by Bill [a cofounder of Numerosity, who is no longer in an executive position with Numerosity] to work for the finance office. Bill's focus was intensively on the numbers. He is an investor at his core.

> We have analyzed the financials of Numerosity's competitors, who increase in number each year. We give the senior executives an in-depth financial drill-down as a preparation for the annual planning retreat.
>
> We? Well, I own the firm, but Numerosity knows that I use a subcontractor from time to time.
>
> My background? I was in military intelligence in the Army National Guard and then was on the CI team at a major national retailer.

Another outsider was interviewed by Carolyn. Marvin is an owner of AMJ Intelligence, a CI firm. Its website indicates it specializes in providing CI to firms selling consumer goods. AMJ lists three co-owners and three other full-time employees. All three owners appear to be working full-time at AMJ. AMJ has been working with Numerosity for three years.

Marvin: We were first hired to do a couple of strategic profiles of Numerosity competitors by Bill for the annual strategic planning retreat three years or so ago, just before they set up their CI team. So, for the current CI team we were a legacy contactor, as we had a multiyear contract to do these profiles. That contract runs out later this year.

From time to time, we do one-off projects, you know, we heard a rumor that this competitor is considering an investment in another company—what is the status, why, etc.? We do perhaps two or three of those per year for the CI team. I assume they reflect questions given them by senior management, but I do not know.

All three of us [the firm's partners] and our staff all have spent time working for other CI, strategy, and financial planning consultants before getting together.

Despite all of these inside and outside efforts, we soon found out that Numerosity did not seem to have an idea of what Numerosity's competitors were doing, at least with respect to CI. Curtis and Marvin, two of the contractors, did not want to discuss what Numerosity's competitors were doing with CI in the IoT space. We could not tell if that was because they did not know anything about that. Ken said later that he understood that "one or two" of their 10 key competitors had CI operations, but said he did not know anything more.

We did some quick digging of our own. John checked the profiles in LinkedIn for Numerosity's competitors, using "competitive intelligence," "strategic intelligence," "competitor intelligence," "technical intelligence," "technology intelligence," and "market intelligence" in the search. We usually do not use "business intelligence" as a search term because most firms use that for data management personnel, and not for CI professionals.

At seven of Numerosity's competitors, John found people with titles or job descriptions using these terms. Also, Carolyn checked various online job sites for open positions with these terms and found two additional competitors looking for employees with intelligence experience. So, we quickly saw Numerosity's competitors are more active in CI than Numerosity thinks they are. In all, perhaps 9 of their 10 current competitors have some internal CI capability or at least some ongoing CI activity. We concluded that lack of focus on competitors represented an additional symptom of overload for the CI team.

We then went back to Vic for a final interview on what he sees the current role of CI at Numerosity to be.

> **Vic:** From my personal experience, the CI team provides a good quality input to the planning process. Their competitor profiles are spot on.
>
> Are those profiles the internal ones we generate? I do not recall. I know we get some profiles from outside firms, but I assume that they are just inputs to our own profiles. As for the [CI] support for R&D [research & development], sales, etc., my client teams seem satisfied.
>
> I scan the newsletter when it comes. It looks ok. No I do not recall any "big hits" we provided in the newsletter.

Give all of this, we felt the best thing was to step back and start from scratch. We first prepared a quick summary of where we found our assignment:

Starting from Scratch

Internal Memo—Not for Distribution

Here are preliminary checklist questions:

1. Does the client need competitive intelligence? How can they tell?
2. Does it need it to identify potential new threats—can CI help? What kinds?
3. Does it need it to identify recurring threats, internal and external—can CI help? What kinds?
4. Could CI have helped it in the past?
5. What does the client expect CI to do for it?
6. What does it do with the CI it gets now? How useful is it?
7. Are its competitors doing CI? How effectively?

What Are the Answers?

Start with the first question, "Does the client need CI?" The short answer is yes. Our interviews and research indicate that a substantial majority of its competitors already have some CI capabilities. Unfortunately, the client does not realize the extent of that effort. The good news is that they instinctively realize that they need CI: this Assignment came in as a "look at the entire CI process" while "things are still fluid here."

The second question is about using CI to identify potential external threats. Our interviews and research indicate three critical things: first, already Numerosity goes up against a lot of direct competitors; second, the client **must** expect more competitors in the future; third, its existing competitors will continue to develop, that is get bigger, better, more complex, or just get out.

The third question is whether Numerosity needs CI to identify and deal with recurring threats, and, if so, what kinds? Already Numerosity uses CI in its annual planning process, as well as for current awareness. It also uses it for sales and for R&D.

Fourth, Numerosity's use of CI is so ambiguous that we have no way of determining if it could have helped in the past, but the failure to catch the Canadian government's decision over three years ago to leave the market certainly seems to indicate it certainly could have and should have.

As for the fifth question, the very existence of this assignment means that the client still does not know what it wants CI for.

Sixth, our interviews indicate that the client does not make much use of the CI it gets now.

The client was not able to answer the seventh question about its competitors CI efforts at all accurately. That indicates a major void.

Reviewing this, we became concerned that the client is somewhat separate from its own CI process. Even our individual client contact, Vic, is just a place keeper for a new CFO. Of course, that assumes that the CI unit at Numerosity should continue to report to the CFO, which is also questionable at this point.

We returned for additional interviews. We now conducted one with the CEO of one of the SBUs, Gaye, while talking with Margaret.

Margaret: As you can see, at Numerosity, we have historically followed a model with extensive use of contract employees and outsourcing. I mean, in the CI area, we have only three people covering the holding company so they use several outside contractors. That model worked for the first stages of our growth, but we must move away from that. Over time, I would like to see Numerosity develop as a true holding company, in charge of overall strategy and finance, with most other functions pushed down to the SBUs.

John: That is interesting. We saw a hint of that with respect to the CI newsletter.

Margaret: Really? The newsletter? I do not usually read that. Anyway, as I was saying, that is something that Vic is digging more deeply into.

Vic: The reason we asked Helicon to come in is that we are looking at this very issue. We have to bring more inside the walls, that is, do less contracting out. And CI is just a part of that total effort.

That is particularly an issue with "independent contractors." As the past shows—you remember the issues with Microsoft, the IRS, and related lawsuits years ago—when you use too many of these and manage them too much like regular employees, you can have legal and tax problems. And I think that is still a potential issue throughout the high-tech community.

As for using contract employees, which you have not suggested, but which I have been considering, I think that should only be a transition strategy at best. If they are good enough to work with us, they should be permanent. Otherwise, when the end of the contract looms near, they are focusing on getting the next contract or into next company instead of on their work for us.

While Numerosity has traditionally promoted from within, in the long run that puts us at the mercy of a very small personnel pool. In fact, I have not seen a lot of movement of people from the SBUs up to corporate. The only fresh blood at corporate has been affirmatively brought in by the founders, which I think is a recognition that this generation of corporate development has to get less insular. That has to continue to change if this is going to be an integrated entity which is the way we will be going. And that is for all functions, not just intelligence.

Gaye: Now, I realize that we sometimes need outside contractors for intelligence. We have and should use them for one-off projects, to provide peak capacity, and to bring expertise that we can learn from to new and complex tasks. Also, I can see contracting out things like benefit management, that sort of thing, which needs expertise, but where it may not make sense for us to develop and nurture it. But it takes time to find and deal with a contractor, and we have issues of confidentiality, conflicting assignments, that sort of thing, which you can avoid by staying inside our own four walls. That is, it seems to me, especially true for intelligence as well as things like strategy development.

Conflicting assignments? By that I mean hiring a firm which has worked for a competitor or which may do so after our retention. I don't think we should work with one currently working for a competitor—ever! And maybe not even if it worked for one in the past—I am not sure about that.

I know having worked for a competitor can mean that it may be more experienced, or can be faster to come up to speed, but what happens after we finish? How much of what we know or learned can move, even imperceptibly, to another competitor? I do not believe that this issue in the strategy, merger and acquisition, and product development areas receives enough scrutiny. But it bothers me. I think that is an issue we should deal with in the competitor, sorry competitive, intelligence process. I do not know what are the operating issues there, but I want us to be forewarned and forearmed.

Our interviews continued to reveal a sense of vagueness, for lack of a better word, about the use of CI at Numerosity. Frankly, it seems to have backed into it. It is working fairly well for Numerosity, but it is just a kind of background process. Numerosity gets both a low-value product—a newsletter—and good support for its annual planning—traditionally a high-value product. The rest of the work of the CI team seems to be behind the scenes, that is, no senior officer or even the CI unit director could name any major efforts or projects. The Numerosity's CI team is experienced, but self-taught—and that imposes real limits on it.

Numerosity does not seem to have a handle on what competitors are using CI, much less how effectively. In fact, we did not get the sense that they were even aware of the fact that a competitor of one of their SBUs was getting out of the United States, which they should have known just from a routine announcement of an executive change where that decision was linked to its pending "consolidation into the Canadian market." It was that three-year-old event that was just mentioned, without comment, in the newsletter.

At this point, the Assignment had several elements. One is the fact that the client is seeking a complete review of its CI operations, so nothing is off limits. Another is that the client seems committed to CI, but does not seem to be getting real value out of it. And third, it does not seem to be aware of that void.

Because Numerosity's CI operations are almost on autopilot, we were very concerned that there are other significant blind spots. We know they are looking at their competitors, but they are not looking out for new competitors, not worrying about suppliers that could become competitors, that sort of thing. Numerosity needs to develop a way to identify its real CI needs—that is, intelligence that they need to know, not just what is nice to know. That is absent in its current operations.

Solutions

Before we went any further, Ken announced that he was leaving the firm to accept a financial analyst position with a firm not in this market space. Vic's replacement as CFO was also named, but before that, Margaret, the CEO announced that the CI function would continue to report to Vic, but in his capacity as COO.

With some personnel issues now stabilized, we returned to the overall assignment, as usual, reviewing where we were before putting our thoughts down on paper to make them more precise for our discussions with the client.

We saw that there were still several personnel issues. The first is that there is a culture where there are several sets of people, with different origins, who are not well meshed:

- There are the original Numerosity people who are still there. They feel grounded and that they "own" the business.
- Then there are the "newbies" who came in with each acquisition. There has been almost no effort to integrate them into the parent company or vice versa.
- A third group is the upper level managers who replaced the founders. Their interviews indicated that they are still trying to find their way. Some of these managers appear to realize that there are several cultures, while others may not. From our conversations with the staff and senior managers, we think that many of them feel that there must be more integration of the SBUs and Numerosity than there is.

Carolyn: Is this culture a problem for our work in CI? Remember, our job is not to fix an entire company—even if it is dysfunctional. At best, we should let the client know that we see these problems if they will make the CI unit and its operations dysfunctional or even impossible.

John: It is not dysfunctional. In the very near future, management will be moving people around to fully integrate them. And that fits what we need in CI.

The second personnel issue is that Numerosity has relatively untrained people with broad intelligence responsibilities, working in an integrated CI unit. And the quality of the CI being generated did not appear to be sterling, to say the least. The newsletter is not much—and its reception is not much either. In fact, we could not find anyone who thinks the newsletter is great.

A few think it is "ok" and gives them "good background." In other words, at best it is good to know, not need to know—not actionable intelligence.

We did not change our tentative conclusion that, if the client keeps the newsletter, and that is still up in the air, it should be contracted out, and the CI personnel should focus on monitoring it and generating occasional alerts themselves.

As for the rest of the CI that was produced, the CI unit is seen as producing "useful" CI, but not intelligence that is "mission critical," to put it in Numerosity's own terminology.

As for DIYers, from what we have seen and heard, there are a couple of them in the some of the SBUs. They are doing their own CI out of what they perceive as a lack of corporate support, the most common reason for that occurring in any firm.

At that point, we decided to write up a draft report. Then we will sit down with the client and relate what we have found. They wanted a face-to-face briefing, not a PowerPoint or long memo, so the memo would be for our use only.

With respect to the cultural conflict issues, the client seems to be dealing with them, so we wanted to make sure that our recommendations fit with and do not conflict with that process. To be effective, CI has to be a part of the organization and not merely something bolted on.

Internal Checklist

This is the text of our internal checklist for this part of the CI rescue process at Numerosity:

Numerosity Project—Draft Summary—Internal and Not for Distribution
1. Show Numerosity where intelligence can help them and begin to do so
   a. What options do you face?
      i. Create CI activities—1,2, or 3 of these options:
         1. Centralized CI team
         2. Decentralized CI
         3. DIY CI
      ii. Replace/redirect the CI activities? Any or all these options:
         1. Change reporting relationships
         2. Change targets
         3. Change focus—competitors' tactics versus strategies, suppliers versus customers versus competitors
         4. Change deliverables—the kind of CI is being provided drives how it is to be delivered
         5. Replace/retrain/add to CI personnel
         6. Supplement CI team with DIYers

      7. Educate internal customers on how better to ask for and use CI

      8. Add/change review and feedback processes

   iii. Close down or reposition existing CI activities? Options are 1, 2, or 3 of the following:

      1. Eliminate it entirely?

      2. Use outside resources—partially or entirely

      3. Encourage/require DIY CI

         A. By whom

         B. Focused on what?

2. The correction (putting the CI rescue into practice)

   a. Where do you start?

      i. CI team

      ii. DIYers

     iii. Customers

     iv. Senior management

   b. What processes get fixed and when?

      i. Reporting relationships

      ii. Targets

     iii. Focus—competitors' tactics versus strategies, suppliers versus customers versus competitors

     iv. Deliverables

      v. Replace/retrain/add to CI personnel

     vi. Supplement CI team with DIY CI

    vii. Educate customers

   viii. Review and feedback processes

We will propose what we see as a necessary restructuring of the CI activities as follows:

- Option 1: At the corporate level, assign a CI team of one or two persons to strategy and holding company operations. These duties will include preparing and running war games as well as potentially conducting early warning activities. Move the balance of CI personnel to the individual SBUs.

- Option 2: Leave the CI unit intact, with it still reporting to the COO. Returning it to reporting to the CFO gives it the appearance of being strictly "number crunchers."

With respect to CI staff, we recommend:

- Formal training on CI for all existing and new CI staff. Those now in Numerosity have little or none. All new hires or internal assignees should also have training from outside sources. The in-house CI staff should also set up internal training/education sessions at some of their regular meetings. The goal is to improve the quality of the work and to assure that no one misses key intelligence nuggets. They can also deal with related issues like protecting the firm against the competitive intelligence actions of competitors.

- The CI staff training and meetings should focus the CI staff's attention on developing and delivering actionable CI. The nature of competition is such that not only will the targets change but the vital intelligence Numerosity needs will change as well.

- Begin developing a strong feedback process. The internal CI customers should see that participating in that will make sure that the CI they get in the future will be actionable, timely, and vital. There is no real feedback now, so the CI personnel do not know what their customers need and the customers do not know what the CI personnel can provide to them.

- No one has indicated any problems with the existing outside CI contactors. But experience suggests avoiding reliance on a sole outside source. The firm should maintain at least two credible firms as sources for additional research and analysis at the corporate level, and possibly for each SBU. Whether there is sufficient work to warrant a retainer is not clear—right now there does not seem to be a need, particularly with the client's aim at building up internal capabilities and minimizing outside contracting.

With respect to non-CI personnel, we recommend:

- Training the internal consumers of CI on how to be better clients. Frankly, after the CI personnel have been (re)trained, they can and should do this themselves. Remind them that it is good outreach and career development for them. We have already provided templates for this in *The Manager's Guide to Competitive Intelligence* and *Proactive Intelligence*.

- Reaching out to find all the CI DIYers present in the SBUs. These operations do not have their own CI personnel—yet. They rely on the corporate team for what CI they get. It is very probable that there are some more DIYers there. They should be approached and brought into the CI process as they can help the full-time CI personnel in providing vital intelligence nuggets from their own work.

After a review with Vic, we then made these final, detailed recommendations.

Mission of the CI Unit

The client faces a competitive environment that is and will continue to be subject to rapid change. In addition, when informally benchmarked against its current competitors, it appears to be significantly weaker in its CI efforts. The CI unit is also held back by its history within the client.

The CI should be positioned to directly serve all senior-level officers, as well as the R&D and sales units:

For the senior-level officers, it should continue to provide significant intelligence on competitors, including for the planning process, but without relying on the profiling system currently in place. That system uses up significant internal and external resources while generating a static product. That is, the product quickly loses its relevance with the passage of time, but the profiles are updated only once a year.

The strategic intelligence needed by the senior officers is and will continue to be more dynamic in nature. To provide what the senior officers need, the CI unit should meet regularly directly with them, in addition to meetings with the planners, to determine "what keeps them up at night." These internal customers cannot be expected to tell the CI unit what to look for when unpredictable change is a constant. Rather, the CI unit has to be empowered to search continually for events, changes, and the like, which may impact the firm. Then it must communicate that intelligence, clearly explaining its significance and likely impact on Numerosity and its SBUs.

For the R&D unit, the CI unit will have to learn how to provide significant competitive technology intelligence (CTI). That will entail learning more about the technologies involved in the IoT space, as well as developing and exploiting potential interviewees in industry, the media, regulators, and the academic community to spot and then track what is coming before it becomes what has happened.

For the sales force, the CI unit will have to work directly with the sales force, building up confidence with the sales force so that the sales persons quickly share data, even rumors, with the CI unit. That sharing will help the CI unit to be able to develop tactical intelligence to help the sales team, as well as helping the CI unit in its developing CTI and strategic intelligence for its other internal customers.

The CI unit should issue intelligence alerts only as needed. These should be short, clear, identify the key issues in SWOT terms, and provide a brief analysis of both what is known and what can be developed later. These alerts should always refer the customers back to the CI unit for additional assistance.

TRAINING AND STAFFING LEVELS

With Ken's planned departure, Numerosity needs to hire a new CI manager, or to promote one from within.

In the first option, the client must fully articulate the mission of the CI unit before bringing on any new hire. That is because the current personnel culture will make it difficult for an outsider to implement rapid change after coming in and taking charge.

In the second option, that is, promoting from within, a new manager will need to reach out to the newly expanded internal client base to develop a new sense of what the CI unit will be doing. Its past position and work products might create concern among its new and existing clients about its ability to help, which the CI unit will have to face and overcome.

Given the current and anticipated future work load, the CI unit should be expanded. Recognizing the current personnel culture, that would seem to mean adding someone from within Numerosity or one from the SBUs, but recognizing that means adding someone who lacks any formal, significant CI background or experience to a team already lacking in such training.

Because of that, the remaining members of the unit, and all new additions, including the new manager, will need significant training. Learning about CI on the fly is never sufficient—it is rarely even satisfactory. There are several options that are not mutually exclusive:

Hire an outside CI specialist to train the CI unit on site and possibly serve as an ongoing mentor for a fixed period. Such retention should not be with a firm on the approved outside contractor list. That might raise questions of propriety or at least concerns by other firms on that list that one firm "has the inside track."

Have all CI unit members attend third-party onsite or offsite training. Such courses are offered by a variety of associations and firms in the United States and Europe. Some aim at granting a formal certification; others do not. One option would be for individuals mix and match—that is, have two attend some courses from supplier A, then split them up and send each to courses from different suppliers, B and C, etc. The goal is to expose the entire group to the widest possible scope of resources. Added training options may be also available locally at the university level.

Have CI unit members attend CI and other intelligence-focused sessions at trade association meeting and other conferences they usually attend. Then, have an individual who attended the session report back to the team on the session and its key learnings.

NEWSLETTER

The client should end the production of the existing newsletter. As it is now, it diminishes the reputation of the CI process while consuming valuable resources while providing no actionable intelligence.

If senior management and the heads of the SBUs still want a newsletter, it should be contracted out, with final responsibility for editorial management left with the CI unit. Before it is contracted out, the CI unit must work with the contractor to see that the contractor has a hard focus on providing vital, timely, and concise information. As the CI team is not handing over full responsibility for this, but rather just freeing up skilled staff time, this project should be protected from the overall policy against contracting out.

If the newsletter is still to be produced internally, the sales personnel should be brought into the newsletter process by having them responsible for generating some editorial content on a regular basis.

Outside Contracting

With a new head of the CI unit in place, the contracts with the four outside contractors should be reviewed. The first thing should be to find out if there are any potential conflicts of interest. That is, have any of the firms worked for others in the IoT industry? Numerosity should make sure that these past retentions did not generate a conflict of interest. Are any of them now working for a firm in the IoT industry? If so, relations with such a firm should be terminated.

When using an outside firm, Numerosity should watch out for blind subcontracting. In blind subcontracting, the firm taking a contract then gives some or all the contract work to another individual or firm, that is, someone other than an employee or subsidiary, but without notifying the client. If the client is uncomfortable with this, and it should be, it should make sure that its contracts protect it from this from the beginning.

The new CI manager should determine what parts, if any, of the competitor profiles previously provided by the CI unit were actually produced in-house, and which were actually done by outside contractors and just incorporated into the CI unit's work product. At the same time, the end users of these profiles should be surveyed or otherwise interviewed to determine how they used them, when they used them, and what elements should be added or deleted. At that point, the new CI manager can decide if this work is sufficiently valuable to be kept in-house or if outside assistance is sufficiently valuable to warrant contracting out a small part.

In keeping with the CEO's vision on contracting out, this means that most existing third-party contracts would be run out or just ended. That is not to say that the client should never contract out intelligence research. But it can provide for such needs in the future by pre-clearing two or three firms for such efforts. Then, when a need arises, the CI manager can make sure that there are no current conflicts of interest, and proceed. Any such lists should be refreshed every three–four years by adding new members and removing others.

What happened at the client after we were done? How successful were we?

Not surprisingly, Numerosity quickly promoted one of the CI team members to replace Ken. It also made the unit directly report to the COO. Following this, Numerosity then added three members to the CI unit. While it did not go outside for new hires, it did turn to the SBUs to recruit these three individuals. One recruit had experience in strategic planning, one in R&D, and one in sales support. None had any CI experience or any CI training.

Numerosity then told us it would arrange for all members of the new CI unit to attend training. In keeping with the new training regimes that the COO installed for all employees, each member will attend one multiday course each year as well as at least one session at a conference or trade show dealing with some aspect of CI. A part of the new corporate training regime, also just introduced, is the use of the "hand-off." That meant that each person who got training or went to a session had to make a short presentation to all his/her peers about what was valuable in the course or session. These presenters were then evaluated both on the content they provided to their team and on their now improving communication skills.

Reaching out to the senior officers was quickly facilitated by a new requirement that a member of the CI unit be designated as a required attendee at all planning, budgeting, and business development meetings. A working relationship with R&D took longer to create, due to the complexity of the work being done there, although assigning the unit member with a technical background cut the learning time down substantially. It quickly became evident that the demands for intelligence from the R&D team were significantly higher than anticipated. Numerosity is now exploring imbedding CTI staff in each SBU; while there, they will continue to work directly for the CI unit.

Work with the sales force is progressing much more slowly. Many of the sales staff members are reluctant to share any information with anyone outside of the sales force, and, it appears, even within the sales force. This cultural attitude is somewhat reminiscent of the initial problems we had with Ken about sharing information with us. Fortunately, the sales managers are now aware of the problem of sharing, which they believe have also negatively impacted sales efforts, and are working on it. When that process is completed, the CI unit will try again to work with the sales force.

One unexpected glitch was that a few of the officers in the SBUs did not like the elimination of the newsletter—so the client eventually brought it back. But the CI team is working to improve both its content and timeliness. Members of the CI unit rotate taking care of it, adding a brief analytical note to major items. Due to the obstructive culture within the sales force, there is still no section in the newsletter from them. The CI team probably will not contract the newsletter out in the future. Numerosity is now moving even firmly away from any significant contracting out. The newsletter had been contracted out for the short term, and now internal again, is issued by the CI team on a weekly basis.

In keeping with the overall policy on sharply reducing the use of outside contractors, Numerosity has quickly brought all existing CI work in-house. After our suggested review, the CI team is no longer developing the previous annual profiles for distribution; instead it maintains these profiles, and regularly updates them, but for their own reference. These profiles help the CI team in responding to intelligence requests.

After interviews and reviewing past work by its existing contractors, the CI unit has also generated a list of three firms, each preapproved to compete for CI research assignments. Only one of the existing firms was put on that list.

LOOKING BACK ONE YEAR LATER

Later, we found that Numerosity was sending all the CI staffs to commercial CI courses in the United States and in Europe. Only two at a time are going to the courses; the internal training people were also "sampling" the available training vendors for larger on-site training work in the future. So, over time, the current CI staff members will get training from a variety of vendors. Numerosity has left it to the CI team members to decide what sessions to attend at annual industry and intelligence conferences. The client's belief is that this will improve their knowledge base and that of the entire team by exposing them to different points of view.

As the CI team has matured and received its additional training, Numerosity is using its CI team to train other employees in the holding company, and later in the SBUs, on how to protect themselves from the CI efforts of competitors. That was expected to start in six months, but within five months, the CI team was already running a successful internal course on protecting Numerosity and its SBUs against the CI efforts of competitors. The course, presented in co-operation with corporate security personnel, is now offered at least twice a year. All present corporate and SBU officers were initially required to attend within the next two years. All new manager-level hires across the board must attend the course as soon as possible after being hired.

To cover all the other existing employees—Margaret has decided that all employees must eventually be educated on these defensive concepts—Numerosity is working with Helicon to develop its own internal, online course, which eventually will be available to all employees. Those not required to attend the live course must take it online within 15 months of its launch. All those who have attended a live course must take a shorter, review version of the course every 30 months.

Here too the "culture" issue raised its head, with some officers who came in with acquisitions resisting taking the live course. Margaret eventually changed the criteria for taking the live course, allowing existing officers to take the online course as an option. However, anyone promoted to an officer position must take a live course within a year of assuming the position.

The CI process is rapidly maturing at Numerosity.

8

Integrating an Acquisition, Developing DIY Capabilities, and Adding Primary Research Capabilities

THE CASE

About the Company

Blanford Controls is a large, privately owned research, development, and controls manufacturing firm. Its manufacturing operations rely heavily on its internal R&D operations, although it does do contract manufacturing of prototypes for companies in the aerospace, controls, and related sectors.

All its operations are in the same state, within a 10-mile radius of headquarters. These operations include the headquarters office facility, two R&D centers, a manufacturing plant, and a prototype production center.

In 2003, Blanford began a series of small acquisitions, purchasing private R&D operations to acquire their top R&D personnel. To date, it has made four such acquisitions. We were not told if there are more pending when we started this assignment.

Its Management, Owners, and Employees

Blanford has been in business since 1946. Its earliest days of operation were as a subcontractor for a variety of large defense firms. In the late 1950s, it began to develop its own R&D functions. By the 1980s, the bulk of its revenues came from contract R&D, that is, R&D done for other firms. In 2002, Blanford began to do specialty and prototype manufacturing, making products based on its own research as well as that done by others.

Currently, there are over 100 individuals working in Blanford's R&D function. Their higher education runs the gambit from two-year technical school through doctoral degrees from major university engineering and physics programs. The most senior of them are designated as "technology managers."

The company is employee-owned, so all full-time employees share in an annual profit distribution. About 50 percent of its upper management has come up from within, largely through the R&D function. That group includes the current CEO, Willis. The balance of its senior management has been recruited from government labs and from domestic competitors.

Blanford recruits most of its R&D and of its manufacturing personnel from recent graduates of local colleges and universities and provides substantial post-hire training for all its employees. It has a 3-decade-old education program that pays for advanced technical and technology education, and even advanced degrees, in some cases, for its employees. The result is that Blanford has a very low employee turnover rate.

A Look at Its Competitive Environment and Market Profile

Blanford regards itself as very conservative. It has invested and continues to invest significantly in hiring and retaining the talent in its R&D operations to keep most work inside. However, it does partner with R&D firms throughout the world on larger projects. It is highly regarded in its market space and seeks to utilize the most advanced scientific techniques. Its clients still include some U.S. companies in the defense industry, but, since 2002, it has widened its scope of business. Now it does business throughout North America and Western Europe.

As it has made acquisitions, it has also generated competitors. Over the past four years, five individuals associated with past acquisitions have left Blanford. one set up a small R&D firm, with which Blanford now does some contract work. The other four have joined government contractors, largely, but not exclusively, in the defense marketplace. Previously, they were clients of Blanford with respect to their nongovernment business. That is no longer the case. These firms are now direct competitors of Blanford for some non-government business.

As with other firms doing substantial business directly or indirectly with governments, Blanford's business from this sector has been relatively flat in the past several years. However, its work with private firms in the energy and infrastructure sectors has grown, although not steadily. Its prototype manufacturing operations, while state-of-the-art, have been seeing slow-downs due to the increased usage of and rapidly declining costs of prototyping techniques, driven by such technologies as fused deposition modeling (FDM). FDM is an additive manufacturing technology used for modeling, prototyping, and other production applications. Importantly for Blanford, it is one of the techniques currently used for its 3D printing.

What were its plans? What is coming next?

Blanford is closing on its largest acquisition so far, Vills, Ltd., a firm that is about 25 percent of Blanford's size. Vills is primarily a prototyping firm, but has a very strong R&D reputation. Blanford will be signing employment contracts with the R&D personnel at this firm at the closing, as Willis, its CEO says, to "prevent brain drain like in the past."

Vills is a U.K.-based firm, but the bulk of its operations are in the United States, including all its R&D activities. One attractive element for Blanford was that Vills' U.S. operations are only about 50 miles from Blanford's headquarters, so Blanford does not see any problems with integrating it quickly and completely.

Status of Intelligence Operations

At present, Blanford has no formal CI activities, but relies on its technology managers for the CI that it uses. In the United States, Vills has a two-person team conducting CI for its R&D unit and its U.S. sales team. The Vills personnel were both trained as special research librarians. Vills does not have any CI personnel in the United Kingdom supporting its operations there.

What problems/issues were identified by the client?

We started with a meeting with Willis, Blanford's CEO.

Willis: In the past, we have been doing ok in terms of intelligence on what technology our competitors are developing or dealing with because our R&D people are "wired in" to a lot that goes on in the industry. However, recently we have found that we are not as on top of this as we thought we should be. Part of that was that our new hires gradually lose contact with the networks they built up at universities. Also, after some digging, we realized that we were getting some of this intelligence, a lot really, from new employees who came in with each new acquisition. That is, the people we brought onboard were already networked into the cutting edge of critical developments.

However, after they had been here for a while and become a part of our team, the value of their old network quickly diminished. These things tend to dry up, in part because we do not like our people to attend a lot of conferences where the competition can try and "chat them up." We are going to have to look at that too. Any thoughts you have there will be appreciated.

Also, we lost a couple of key people from the acquisitions after they were here for a while, so their networks are completely gone, too. It all, sort of, well, aged out. So, we have to do something to replace this that does not involve making a new purchase every two—three years.

Speaking of acquisitions, there is the Vills' acquisition coming up to its closing. In the U.K., this is just a small sales operation. A lot of its other operations were sold off last year, if I recall, to a German firm, leaving them with, essentially, a U.K. sales office and good-sized R&D [research and development] operations with a few sales people here in the U.S. Anyway, this is what we purchased.

The Vills' U.S. operations have a CI team in place. Vills is relatively happy with them. But, excuse me, and off the record, "librarians"? I do not think that is good enough. But I cannot do anything there yet, not until the acquisition finally closes in six–eight weeks. But I think we have to look at beefing this up.

So we need intelligence help at the company level, help with Vills once that closes, and also help in linking them together with whatever we do at the parent company level.

At this company, we believe in teamwork and really depend on keeping our personnel for the long haul, so I am not looking to replace people, including those now at Vills, but to upgrade them and to make them better. That, in the long run, makes us all better, too.

OUR PERSPECTIVES

Key CI Diagnostic Quiz Results

How is the current and future CI team staffed, trained, and managed?

Yes

Both Blanford technology managers and the Vills team have current industry knowledge.

Maybe/Possibly

The incoming Vills team may understand the CI processes in which they participate.

No

The Blanford technology managers have no specific training on CI, and it appears that the incoming Vills team has no such training either.

Blanford's technology managers do not understand the CI processes in which they participate.

How do the technology managers and the future CI team get direction on targets, on its data collection, and on deliverables?

Yes
Technology managers at Blanford are responsible for providing some or all their own CI.

Maybe/Possibly
The Vills team may have a systematic process for identifying and defining Vills' intelligence needs.

No
Blanford's CI program does not meet its users' needs on an ongoing basis.
Blanford's technology managers do not have a systematic process for identifying and defining their intelligence needs.

Where do technology managers and the future CI team get its data?

Maybe/Possibly
The Vills team probably uses secondary sources of information (public materials, analysts' reports, etc.) to learn about key competitors and/or new products and technology.

No
Technology managers at Blanford have not developed external networks to assist in their data gathering.

What intelligence do technology managers and the future CI team provide?

Maybe/Possibly
The Vills team may systematically collect, analyze, and disseminate intelligence to those people in the firm responsible for business planning and decision-making.

No
Blanford's intelligence program does not systematically collect, analyze, and disseminate intelligence to those people in the firm responsible for business planning and decision-making.

What does our firm do to help our CI process?

Yes
Management is making visible efforts both to support and to use CI.
Blanford recognizes CI as a legitimate and necessary activity in today's marketplace.

No
Blanford does not ensure that technology managers are provided professional education in the areas they are primarily responsible, such as data collection and analysis.

What do its managers and executives expect from and get from technology managers and the future CI team?

Maybe/Possibly

Technology managers at Blanford may expect CI to have a tangible and measurable impact on company decisions and business performance.

No

Blanford's CI program is not run by people professionally trained to produce CI for the management unit's varying needs.

What results has the CI process achieved at the firm?

No

Blanford cannot identify the past and current impacts of the CI process.

What were the real problems there? Why are they different from what the company said they were?

Lack of External Intelligence

Blanford's CEO was spot on about several of the firm's problems. He was correct about the firm's past sources of CI and why that flow has fallen off. One thing he is missing, though, is that Blanford significantly contributes to its own problems. By withholding its employees from external meetings, conferences, and the like, it also cut off their ability to develop and maintain the external networks so useful to developing CTI by themselves. To turn that around, the R&D employees at Blanford could, with some training, begin to provide some of the CTI that Blanford knows it needs.

Willis' concerns about having these employees become targets of the CI collection efforts of competitors are well-founded. But the solution to his problem is not to keep Blanford's employees away. The solution lies in training them on basic elicitation techniques. Not only would that permit them to spot and protect themselves from these competitor CI collection efforts. It might also enhance their own interviewing skills, thus improving their own intelligence "take" from these meetings and conferences.

And, encouraging employee attendance at such meetings, instead of cutting them off, might also minimize, or even eliminate, the turn-over issue with respect to technical employees who joined the firm from past acquisitions, but then left. It is our experience that technical and scientific personnel want and need to keep up their contacts with people and trends in their fields.

Integrating the New CI Team

Since the new unit, Vills, already has a CI team, one option is to move the two members physically to the parent company after the closing. If the commute is too long, Blanford can use telecommuting; that is already being used effectively with many corporate CI teams whose members are geographically scattered.

Willis' concern about the skills of the employees at Vills is very also savvy, although based on limited information. What should be his concern is not that they are librarians, but rather that they may rely, perhaps 100 percent, we do not yet know, on secondary research for the data for their intelligence analyses. To provide first-rate, actionable analyses, they should either be trained to do their own interviews, including elicitation interviews, and/or to work closely with the technical staff in R&D, which can serve as a primary research resource for them.

However, that still leaves the Vills sales force without a CI resource. We will have to dig deeper to see if that will be an issue for Blanford as well. We suspect it probably is.

Coordinating Meeting the CI Needs of Blanford and Vills After the Acquisition

Given the recommendation to move the Vills CI team to Blanford headquarters, where they will meet the CI needs of Blanford and Vills' R&D personnel, these personnel should be sent to basic CI courses, which are also to be taught to the technology managers at Blanford. This will support their own DIY activities as well as those of the CI managers at Blanford.

To assure close cooperation with the (soon to be) corporate CI team, we may suggest that the course be presented or copresented by the in-house CI team. That has historically generated a good bond when major changes in CI are being instituted. It changes the possible "us versus them" to "all of us in this together."

Since the Vills purchase has not closed, we cannot interview its sales force to find out how effective the existing CI duo is in supporting their work, if they do that at all. We can only try and make some forward-looking recommendations to Willis for dealing them once the sale is closed.

Where and how did we solve the client's real problems and help the client?

Lack of External Intelligence and Defending against Elicitation at Conferences

Before working on a plan for the technology managers at Blanford, as well as those joining from Vills, we first interviewed the director of R&D at Blanford, Nina. Nina has been with Blanford for 10 years, having joined the firm after finishing her MS in micro-engineering. Since joining Blanford, she has also earned an MS in materials science through its education and training program.

Carolyn: How many technology managers does Blanford have now?

Nina: Right now—about 35 that are full technology managers. We also have associate managers and associates, about 65 of them. But that does not include the dozen or two that will be joining us with Vills.

Carolyn: How many meetings do they attend each year? By that I mean technical conferences, trade shows, and the like.

Nina: Not very many. We tend to send the sales force to the trade shows to represent us, with three or four technology managers on call at the event. We rotate them. We do four or five trade shows in the U.S. each year.

We have had discussions with the technology managers about technical conferences. They really want to attend them—to keep up their skills, their contacts, that sort of thing. The policy here has been largely against that. Will that change?

Carolyn: I do not know yet, but we suspect it will. If we can train your technology managers to protect them against the intelligence gathering actions of your competitors, would you feel more comfortable having them attend these?

Nina: Oh yes. I would like that flexibility. I think it would help our already good employee retention rates. Technology people need to be a part of the current technology development environment—it is like breathing for them.

But we still have to send the sales force to trade shows. They would not be replaced by the technology managers. Sales does the selling and make the closes. I hope we can bring more technology managers though to those events to help the sales people out.

This interview indicates that the sales force almost certainly needs some CI training as well, both on developing CI and on protecting themselves from elicitation interviews at trade shows.

Integrating a New CI Team

While we were not permitted to interview personnel at Vills until after the acquisition closes, we dug into the background of the CI team there. We first checked their memberships, education and training, and work experience by reviewing their profiles in LinkedIn. We also ran an Internet search for current or past resumes using the terms "vita" and "resume" together with their names. We then went to several professional organizations to see if we could check their current membership directories.

Willis was correct that both had degrees in library science and appeared to have been with Vills for about three to four years. Each of the two team members had a LinkedIn profile, and one also had a three-year-old resume we located. Neither of these resources indicated that either had any education in or specific training on CI. In addition, neither appeared to be members of SCIP, an association covering CI, of SLA, the Special Libraries Association, which has a CI division, or of AIIP, an association covering independent information professionals. We concluded, at least preliminarily, that they should start with some basic training on CI, both on secondary research tricks and on elicitation.

Since they would need elicitation interview training, it was not going to be possible for them to run that training as well. Rather, they should take it along with the R&D personnel from Vills. To assist in integration, one or more of the technology managers at Blanford who had already taken the elicitation courses should work with those taking the second iteration of the courses. In fact, we thought that Blanford should probably have Nina run the course for the new employees from Vills.

Coordinating Meeting the CI Needs of Blanford and the New Vills Team After the Acquisition

At this point, we needed to determine what were Blanford's CI needs, if any. Willis has given no indication that they wanted to change the relatively informal system they had—one that relied on the technology managers using their networks and, in the future, attending meetings, to develop and maintain a simple form of early warning about new technology and competitive developments.

We checked with Willis, who indicated that he preferred to keep the old system, which he called a "nonsystem," relying on their technology managers. We pointed out that he was also acquiring a two-person CI team, which we suggested be given the job of staying in contact with the technology managers and collecting their raw data, while putting it in a larger context to be shared with the managers and with senior management. He agreed that this approach made sense. He pointed out that Blanford would be going from 35 to about 43 technology managers, a pretty large group to deal with on a regular basis. He said, after the Vills acquisition was digested, he might consider adding staff to the new corporate CI team.

As for the sales forces of Blanford and Vills, he said he was satisfied with the way they had been operating, but, after digesting the acquisition, he might come back to Helicon to evaluate if CI would help them in the United States and in the United Kingdom, where the old Vills sales team would still be operating.

What new problems did we run into with the client and how did we solve them?

Given that the Vills acquisition would be closing shortly, Willis asked that we postpone any training until we could put all the combined personnel in a course. However, he said that he did not want to "lose any ground," so he asked us to record a mini, self-directed, course on the basics of CI, and another on the highlights of elicitation, both doing it and protecting against it.

Then, we would return to work with the technology managers in small groups for half-day follow-ups. He felt that the new CI team should have sufficient experience to get along without the extra training needed for the technology managers.

We suggested that we provide an optional reading list for those who wanted that. Nina indicated that "this team will try and read all of them— that's the way they grab new knowledge around here." (Note: a current version of that list can be found at www.DIY-CI.com.)

Here are key overheads and presentation comments from that mini course we presented to a few selected technology managers and which Blanford recorded for internal use:

John: The focus here is on your CI tools. There are a wide variety of analytical tools available. However, always pick tools at the end of your work—not at the start. You want to let the data drive selection of which analytical tool(s) you eventually use. Never let the nature of tool limit newly found data's utility—or worse— cause you to ignore it.

Intellectual Blinders—Yes Yours!

- Assumptions
- Presumptions
- Groupthink
- Excessive focus
- Delivered wisdom

Proven Biases in Intelligence Analysis

- The analyst—you—overestimates the accuracy of your own past judgments.
- Your internal "clients" usually underestimate how much they have learned from your past analysis and reports.

- When running a postmortem of an intelligence failure, those in charge usually judge that events were more readily foreseeable than they actually were.

John: There are some proven techniques for starting your research properly. First, step back and define your CI research. Ask yourself, "What specific intelligence am I looking for?" To put it another way, if you today had the intelligence that you are looking for now, what decision would you be able to make now that you cannot make without it? In other words, is it really going to be actionable CI? If you cannot answer this question, refine your task; otherwise, you risk seeking and then getting general information, rather than actionable intelligence. Keep in mind "need to know" versus "want to know."

Limitations and Constraints—Be **Absolutely Honest**

- Just how much time can you devote to this research?
- What resources are available to you?: Money, inside help, outside help?
- The last is your calendar.
  - In addition to how much time you can devote to the work, when you need an answer is another calendar constraint.
  - Remember, it is better to have a pretty good answer on time than a perfect one 2 weeks late.

John: Let's look at legal and ethical limits on competitive intelligence. Above all, keep in mind that they deal with how information is collected. Let's get specific. You cannot steal materials from a competitor, misrepresent for whom you work, or take any number of other dubious, if not illegal, steps.

Now, about ethics: most problems you might face are because of ethical, not legal, missteps. Use this as an ethical rule of thumb: do you want what you did or plan to do reported on the front page of your local paper tomorrow?

A related question deals with trade secrets. The U.S. Economic Espionage Act of 1996 deals with theft of trade secrets, and every state has laws defining trade secrets. To keep it short, if you come into possession of a trade secret of a competitor, immediately contact your attorneys, bring them all the materials that you may have received accidentally or otherwise, and let them handle it from there.

Question: Is there anything else we have to know?

John: Yes. Always check into any written, and unwritten, policies here at Blanford. This is not limited to any Blanford may adopt about CI. You may have policies unrelated to competitive intelligence that may prevent you from calling a competitor.

Managing Your Research

- What do you need first?
- Tier your research
- Linkages
- Secondary before primary
- Try new things
- Just how much data do you really need?

Start with What You *Think* You Know about the Competitor

- What is it doing now?
- What did it do last year?
- Who is in charge?
- Are you sure you *really know* the answers?
- Are you just assuming it?
- Are you relying on its past conduct to predict the future?

Working the Internet

- Regardless which search engine you use first, **always** use a second
- Forces a refocus, a narrowing of your question
- Here is a handout with some rules to help you navigate the Internet—safely.

20 Rules for Doing CI Research on the Internet

1. Not everything you need is on the Internet for **free.**
2. Not everything has been **published** on the Internet for free.

3. Treat the Internet with **caution.**

    Keep virus protection up-to-date and on.

4. **Not everything** on the web can be found using any, or even all, available search engines.

5. Just because something is on the Internet **today** does not mean it will be there tomorrow.

6. **In spite of Rule 5**, some things that are no longer on the Internet are still there: Google's caching & Archive.org.

7. Be careful out there:

    Without "private browsing," you leave traces of your visits to websites.

    Let your IT people know that you are doing your own CI (they may be tracking you).

8. There is no reason why a competitor's website cannot divert some user traffic, say from your firm, away from sensitive areas (based on your ISP address).

9. Think of different ways to narrow the search other than adding more words:

    Are there likely to be business documents that have been circulated outside the target firm? If so, search for PDF files.

    Has the Target likely made presentations to potential customers, suppliers, etc.? Try limiting search to PowerPoint files or going to PowerPoint sites like slideshare.net.

10. Just because you find the same information on several sites does not mean that the information is now confirmed.

11. When you find something particularly interesting on a competitor, take a few seconds and see whether you could find the same **on your firm.**

12. When exploring **blogs**, remember you have no idea who is actually making which posting, or why.

13. When dealing with blogs, particularly dealing with a target firm, be careful about **entering discussions.**

14. Do not rely on the blogs for hard data; use them to **get to hard data.**

15. The Internet can be an incredibly useful place for locating potential **interviewees**: LinkedIn, Facebook & resumes.

16. Not everyone keeps everything **up-to-date all** of the time.

17. Just because a government agency has a site where you can request information under a **Freedom of Information** act does not mean the process is now faster than before the agency went online.

18. **Secondary** data are just that—secondary.

19. Just because you cannot find it on the Internet does not mean it is **not there.**
20. Providing a report of just what you found on the Internet is **not intelligence**; it is not even analysis.

Start by Visualizing Where Raw Data Might Be

- Open-source information: available to everyone, mostly secondary.
  - 80 percent of what is needed
- Open proprietary information: legally obtained through concerted work.
  - 5 percent more of what is needed
- Closed proprietary information: obtained through "gray" activities—legal but ethically questionable
  - 5 percent more

Where Raw Data Might Be (cont.)

- Classified: closely held, extremely valuable information, such as trade secrets where getting it involves "black," that is , illegal, operations.
  - 10 percent of what is needed
- In other words, more than 80 percent of all data you would need to develop CI on a competitor can be accessed without crossing legal or ethical boundaries.

Your Customers, Suppliers, and the Competition—Are They Good Sources of CI?

- Pros
- Cons
- Approaches and issues

From Customers

- Pros
  - Already being approached by your competitors

- Good source of data on current competitor initiatives, pricing, terms, and quality
- Cons
  - Costly to acquire
  - Getting CI from them may interfere with others in the firm doing research on your current/potential customers

Suppliers

- Pros
  - "Our" suppliers—on our side
  - If they are not also suppliers to competitors, may have a handle on competitors' suppliers—help to determine competitors' costs
- Cons
  - May also be "their" suppliers
  - What you ask may be redirected to competitors
  - Not in their interest to provide some data
- Approaches and issues
  - Cooperation—you should help them too
  - Limit your demands, oops, requests—they do not work for you!

From Competitors

- Pro
  - Have complete, correct, and current data
- Cons
  - Why should they share?
  - Must use indirect approaches
- Approaches and issues
  - Your interest may be early warning to them
  - Avoid questionable approaches
  - Monitor websites, trade shows

Question: What about the people right here at Blanford—and in Vills?

John: Great question. Let's talk about networking with people here at Blanford and outside of the firm as well. Having and using your own networks has, time and again, proven to be critical to development of effective CI operations—both for teams and individuals like you.

Successful CI programs all develop and then use decentralized, relationship-based networks. People like you who are also critical in developing CI should follow this practice, both for internal and for external networks.

Question: Why?

John: Networks allow leveraging your limited resources. Your resources are limited, aren't they?

Group: (Laugh).

John: I will start at the beginning. When you look at creating your own network, where should you start? Start where Blanford has and is developing core capabilities, where it is experiencing its greatest competitive threats, and on key business processes. These must always include sales and marketing for at least two reasons: you can provide CI to them, and they can help gather data for you.

Developing a network is not an overnight job. Allow time to develop it and then continue to nurture it. Start out small as this requires person-to-person contact. It never stops—new members need to be brought in to replace departing members. So if you have a good relationship with someone in marketing who is going to retire, get a hand-off to his or her replacement.

Now I will give you a few data gathering hints.

Data-Gathering Tips

- Start with sources of raw data
  - Government and nonprofit sources
  - Private sector sources
  - The media

Finishing Your Research

- You are done when
  - you run out of time/money
  - you reach your deadline
- Before that?
  - When your research has "closed the loop"
    - Each step now takes you back to a previous one

> ◦ You have looked at a good number of sources of each type and are always coming up dry

John: Then draw conclusions. Facts are not intelligence—they are just inputs when developing intelligence.

How to Make Sense of Your Data

- Pay attention to everything you found
  - ◦ And to what is missing!
- Select the right tools—now is the time
- Allow enough time
  - ◦ How much? 2/3 for analysis—1/3 for data gathering is a good rule
  - ◦ Less analysis almost always produces a poorer product
- Watch for disinformation
- How consistent are your data?
  - ◦ Watch for patterns
  - ◦ Find omissions and displacements

Making Sense of Your Data (cont.)

- Assemble the data
  - ◦ Pull together small pieces to make a big picture
  - ◦ Try organizing it by time, backward by time, and by source
  - ◦ But, you do not need all of the pieces to make a picture
  - ◦ Use analysis to fill in the gaps
- Select from available analytical tools and techniques
  - ◦ Do not start by selecting the tools before you do your research

Here are a few things to keep in mind to enable you to draw actionable conclusions:

- Check for anomalies
- Limit, or eliminate, all assumptions
- Review your results for completeness and consistency
- If you have time, try out your results on someone else
- Deliver what you have when it is needed—perfection delivered too late is worthless.

With respect to data collection, we also provided a short memo for the CI and R&D employees to think about outside of the mini course

Data Collection Tips

Do not collect data for the sheer sake of collecting data. If you are going to collect it, then analyze it and use it in a timely manner. Why? There are at least four good reasons:

1. Analyzing raw data long after collecting it is often a waste of not only of your time but also of your financial resources. You know it is dated, so you (hopefully) will first update it before using it. The effort spent collecting it and then later updating it is probably not much different from the effort you would expend just starting from scratch.

2. What is even worse is collecting data when you "have the time," and then reviewing it at a significantly later date without updating it. Why? Intelligence has a half-life, just like radioactive compounds. In CI, that means there is a period of time after which the data you have collected and the CI you generated from it will lose half, and eventually all its value. Take, for example, a banker who is collecting information on interest rates paid by competitor banks. Collecting it today and not analyzing until next week means that he or she has no actionable, useful CI. Why? Because banks usually change interest rates weekly. So, the CI developed from this week and a half old data will automatically be out of date and without any value.

3. If you collect competitor data regularly, you or others in your firm may erroneously assume that somehow you are therefore always "on top of it." Why? Because your focusing on the target is "ongoing." But unless your analysis is also ongoing, you could have a very serious problem of false security.

4. Having only raw data often produces a false sense of security. That is because it supports the misconception that you have everything you need at your fingertips, so it is "just a matter of time until you get the answer." That brings to mind a story told by a friend of ours about a project many years ago. He was called in to help a CI unit improve. He came to headquarters, and was brought to the CI manager. In this pre-Internet era, the manager proudly told him that they just needed some help straightening out the way they ran the unit's analysis and reporting. He then pointed to several file cases (remember those?), which he indicated were filled with reports, catalogs, SEC filings, news clippings, and all sorts of other raw data on the competitors. My friend turned to the CI manager and claims he said "My God man, I'm too late." The lesson: the manager was crippled by having old data that he felt could be valuable, when it merely served to consume too much time in reviewing it.

Elicitation

Following the first self-directed course, we also developed a few overheads on elicitation interviewing, including protecting against elicitation, which were to be added to the online course. Here are those additional overheads and comments:

Elicitation: Apparently ordinary conversation that is skillfully aimed at drawing out key data without alerting the interviewee

- A key part of primary research
  - Usually follows secondary research
    - Identify targets and topics
  - Often used to fill in or confirm critical details
  - Not the same as regular interviewing
- Most often used at meetings and on telephone calls

John: Before we quickly cover the basic techniques of elicitation interviewing, it will help if I outline its five underlying principles:

- People want to be polite and helpful.
- People answer questions even from relative strangers—remember, for some people, that is their job. That is one reason the "downstream hand-off" works. This is getting one person to refer your enquiry to a subordinate, who feels compelled to talk with you, since your enquiry comes from "upstream" from them.
- People want to seem well-informed about what they do. That tempt them into saying too much.
- People want to be appreciated. They want to feel important and knowledgeable, and to communicate to others their importance/knowledge. That may result in talking even more to you after (gentle) praise about importance or value of their work.
- People are open and honest. That makes them reluctant to withhold information, to lie, or be overly suspicious of someone else.

Now, let's go to some basic techniques.

Techniques

- Direct questions are not usually a good thing
  - People remember them
  - They try to give a yes or no

- Elicitor wants *details*
  - One other goal of elicitor—avoid being remembered
  - Or at least keep subject of conversation from being remembered

Techniques (cont.)

- Keep the conversation moving
  - Shift on and off the subject
- Adopt an attitude that keeps the target talking
  - Gain a connection with the target
  - Constantly acknowledge the speaker
- Use silence as a weapon
  - People do not respond well to it

Techniques (cont.)

- Let the target talk
  - People love to hear themselves talk
  - When they do, they tend to forget other constraints
  - I will give you "5 min" can become a half hour
- Gently provoke responses
  - Challenges
  - Criticisms
  - Corrections
  - Flattery

Techniques (cont.)

- Control the conversation, but do not dominate it
  - Get the target to focus on, and stay focused on, what you want
- Then, move away from the topic
  - Once you have what you want, change the subject
  - The hourglass in the last 2 minutes—after you have narrowed down the topic and have you answer, broaden it again and move away from your target
  - If possible change the subject

- o The target will tend to recall only the last part of the conversation—make that innocuous
- • Do not push it
  - o Know when to quit—and then stop!

John: Finally, here is the flip side. How to spot someone trying to work you and what to do. Remember this the next time you are at a trade show or professional meeting.

How to Spot and Deal with Elicitation

- • How to spot it
  - o What is missing that should be there: the identity of the elicitor, why he/she called, what exactly is wanted.
  - o What is there that should not be: topics seem to be added to the conversation and the elicitor says less and less.
- • How to deal with It
  - o Break it off—you are not so smart that you can overcome it.
  - o Try to figure out who (is in back of it) and what (they were trying to learn).

What happened at the client after we were done? How successful were we?

The technology managers took the CI course very aggressively. Blanford purchased all the books on the reading list, and the technology managers then circulated the copies among themselves until each of them had read at least three different books, just as Nina predicted.

The CI team also took the course, but said afterwards that they still felt they were uncomfortable doing elicitation interviews. Nina and Willis agreed that their work from secondary sources was good enough to keep them on, but Blanford would flip the usual intelligence process so that the secondary CI went from the CI team to the individual technology managers. They then sent their critical intelligence findings to Nina as they emerged, following any needed primary research, such as "working" a conference (which they would be expected to do).

LOOKING BACK ONE YEAR LATER

About eight months later, Nina contacted Helicon to arrange for a short course for the technology managers on how to "work" a meeting or conference. Here is the speaker's outline we used in a recorded session that applied these principles specifically to situation facing the first trade show that the technology managers planned to "work."

Outline: Strategy on Working Trade Shows

- You, the technology managers, must make your number one objective at the trade show intelligence—not direct sales.
- But isn't that what the sales force going there for?
- Deal with this conflict early and work it out.

Step 1—Three–six months out

- Pick the attendee(s).
- Recruit assistance from sales force? Or at least get noninterference agreement.
- Hire outside help?

Step 2—Close to two months before the show

- Formal Training
  ○ Coverage—review and remind everyone.
    - What is CI?
    - What are we looking for at this trade show?
- How are we going to collect the data we need to develop that intelligence? Consider developing a basic form to help those doing interviews.

Step 3—Focus on the event's preliminary schedule

- Review list of confirmed attendees to determine companies, institutions, booths, and people to be targeted.
- Check list of speakers, special presentations, etc. to identify which need coverage
- Assign responsibilities—coach, collectors, booth support, and the like.

Step 4—At the conference—a day before

- What is the objective(s)?
- Who is doing what? Targeting whom? When?
- Review elicitation interviewing techniques.
- Review defensive techniques for your personnel.
- Remind everyone about ethical limits on data collection.

Step 5—Set up the show headquarters

- Central spot for handing in materials and information.
- Each evening, review the day's take and adjust the next day's targeting.
- If possible, everyone should meet there at close of show to capture impressions, suggestions, leads, etc.

Step 6—Assigned roles at the conference

- Coach: in charge of all participants. Must track all attendees and be able to change focus on the fly.
- Collectors:
  - Walk the floor
  - Attend events
  - Interview targets
  - Collecting materials from and photos of, competitors' booths

Step 7—Back at Blanford

- Produce and distribute a final report.
- Start preliminary planning for next event, adjusted in light of intelligence take at this conference.
- Return to Step 1.

Following this course, the technology managers began to work trade shows and their own conferences, at first conservatively, and later, more aggressively. Nina has indicated that the intelligence "take" from these activities is "more than we anticipated." The technology managers report that they enjoyed adding CI to their portfolio. As Willis put it, "Our biggest problem is reminding these managers that their job is still technology, not intelligence."

9

Starting Late

THE CASE

About the Company

Loder's Hardware Store is a small-to-medium-sized hardware store and has been in the Loder family for two generations. The children of Eli, the current owner, are now working there and plan to continue working there.

Loder's is a typical rural hardware store. It carries "a little bit of everything you like," as Eli puts it. It has what Eli calls "the usual hardware stuff: nails, screws, hammers, lumber, electrical stuff, those plug-in saws and things that you use, and so on." They have paint, cleaning, gardening, pet, and seasonal sections. They also have a garden area and a greenhouse. In addition, they rent some equipment from a small area at the back of the store.

Its Management, Owners, and Employees

Eli, the son of the founder, currently owns the store. His two adult children work at the store. Eli expects to leave them the business.

A Look at Its Competitive Environment and Market Profile

Loder's is in a quiet, rural area. Eli says his problem is that the business has been stagnant or even fallen slowly off over the past 10 years although the area has grown and changed. The area has changed because the suburbs have gradually crept out into this area. Right now, there are new homes being built all around the county. Eli feels this gradual growth should be helping his business, but says it has not. Eli thinks that the new homes should represent an increasing market and they are for other existing businesses, but they are not increasing his business.

While he did not mention it when we started, Eli told us later that he felt it that BigBox Hardware would be coming to the county "eventually." So, he was concerned about getting out ahead of them. That is why he called Helicon.

What were its plans? What is coming next?

Eli and his children all expect that the two children will eventually own this store. Eli has not yet given them any idea of when he would retire and turn the store over to them. We asked Eli about that and Eli said he has no idea of when he will retire either. He really seems to have no plans to retire at all. He has no future plans for retirement and no real interest in doing so.

Status of Intelligence Operations

Loder's has no intelligence operations of any sort. As we later found out, Eli actually had an early warning of future competitive problems, but he did not understand it or act on it.

What problems/issues were identified by the client?

Eli says he needs CI to help improve his business, actually to save it:

> **Eli:** I am getting more than a bit desperate. I want a proposal as quickly as possible. Where is my business going?

OUR PERSPECTIVES

Key CI Diagnostic Quiz Results

How is Loder's CI team staffed, trained, and managed?
Loder's has no CI team or other CI capability.

How does Loder's CI team get its direction on targets, on its data collection, and on deliverables?
Loder's has no CI team or other CI capability.

Where does Loder's CI team get its data?
Loder's has no CI team or other CI capability.

What intelligence does Loder's CI team provide?
Loder's has no CI team or other CI capability.

What does Loder's do to help its CI process?
Loder's has no CI team or other CI capability.

What do managers expect from and get from the Loder's CI team?
Loder's has no CI team or other CI capability.

What results has the CI process achieved at Loder's?

Loder's has no CI team or other CI capability.

No

Loder's owner does not use CI at any level of decision-making (i.e., strategic, tactical, budget, planning, etc.).

What were the real problems there? Why are they different from what the company said they were?

The first real problem was that Eli was not paying attention to the real impact of the growth in the area. While new homes continue to be built all around the county, Eli ignored the fact that others, including potential competitors, might also see this as a new area in which to expand their own marketing. Because of that, he had already missed an event that signaled potential new competition.

Where and how did we solve the client's real problems and help the client?

The area around Loder's has changed because of the growth in suburban housing around the county. However, instead of helping Loder's, we found that this area had already drawn the attention of BigBox Hardware. In fact, there was a BigBox in the next county, just across the county line, about 15 miles away. It was possible that it might already be drawing off some of Loder's business.

What new problems did we run into with the client and how did we solve them?

Because CI means knowing about both the competition and potential competition, we targeted the closest BigBox store, in the next county, to check it out. Carolyn reported on her visits on her return.

Carolyn: It is a beautiful store and definitely a big box. It sells everything, including appliances. The relative scale is awesome. Where Loder's sells 4 or 5 brands of wall paint, BigBox sells 25 or more. It has a computerized system that lets you match your paint to anything you can bring in—not just to a paint sample. So, if I want my paint to match one little part of a design in a throw pillow, BigBox can do that for me. Loder's still does its paint matching by eye. The difference is not just in scale; it is in time. Loder's is a throwback in time, a nice one, but still very dated.

Carolyn also drove around, looking for smaller stores similar to Loder's.

Carolyn: There appear to be small stores in that county that are competing successfully with BigBox. What they are doing is like judo. There you do not go directly at a competitor's strength. You avoid that and that puts it off balance. The small businesses there appear to be stressing services, like tool repair, rather than cheap power tool prices. Also, they provide real service. So, for pest control, there is always someone, right on hand, who knows all about the products they carry, and which work best—and worst—for what and where. There was one that even looked like an old-fashioned country store. There, if you needed a bolt for a repair of a swing, you would be taken to the right bin, where the staff member would check the size to make sure it was right, and show you the right nut for it. Compare that with a wall of parts, where you have no one to hold your hand, and must buy six of the parts in sealed container, so you cannot compare their part with your broken one. That sort of difference.

We then decided to see what might be coming into the county, since it seemed clear that Eli had done nothing along these lines. Carolyn stopped by the county offices and chatted up the Planning Commission Secretary. The conversation quickly turned to BigBox. Carolyn soon learned that many locals drove to the next county to shop there now and, in part because of that, BigBox was already planning to build a store in this county. Chatting about this, Carolyn quickly found that BigBox had filed construction plans for a new store in this county.

Like many documents filed with local, state, and federal governments, the site plans and the construction plans for new buildings are available for public inspection and copying. In many local government offices, there is often no need to make a written request to see the files, and then wait for two—four weeks for an appointment. In this county, you can email or even call and make arrangement to review the filing quickly.

Following a follow-up call, the County Planning Commission Secretary showed Carolyn the plans on file, which appeared very similar to the BigBox she had just visited. That is not surprising, but typical of many of the larger chains who have a "one floor plan fits most" philosophy. So, a visit to the neighboring store is almost a look inside the store yet to be built.

According to the Commission Secretary, the needed local approvals were moving through smoothly. That means the new store could be under construction within a month or so and then "open in less than nine months, maybe sooner, from the ground-breaking." It was being tracked by the Commission with considerable interest as the county was looking forward to the increased tax money that the new BigBox will bring to it and to the local government.

With this information in hand, we went back to meet with Eli.

What happened at the client after we were done? How successful were we?

Because of the time frame, that is, with BigBox less than 10 months from being open and competing with Eli, we had no CI proposal we could make to Eli. He is just caught by time and circumstances. If he had been using any CI earlier, he would have had an edge. With that additional time, he might have been able to adapt his business to meet the inevitable huge change in the local competitive environment. However, we felt that all was not lost.

The BigBox Carolyn learned about was just ready to break ground. Eli then noted that it was "not there three years ago, and neither was the BigBox" in the next county. Why did he mention three years? We asked.

> **Eli:** Three years ago, I had an offer for the land on which my store stands—a very good offer. It was from BigBox, well actually it was from some company working for them. My property is not big enough for one of their big retail stores, so I did not pay any attention to it. Also, frankly, I did not want to take it because I wanted my kids to take over the business and they do too.

So, it turned out that Eli had an early warning the BigBox might be coming to the county, but had ignored it. If he had paid attention to that, which was not even CI research, but just evaluating the new facts that came his way, he could have changed his business, maybe even franchised, or just sold the property and done something else. But now, it is too late to do most of that.

We told Eli that BigBox was not just likely to come into the county, but that one would be open nearby in 10 months, based on Carolyn's research at the county office building. Eli said he was hopeful that this warning would allow him to see if that old offer is still on the table so he can salvage something from the coming BigBox threat. He recognized that it probably is not, but "it cannot hurt to find out."

We suggested that Eli look at the businesses already competing, successfully, with BigBox in the adjacent county. From our perspective, it seemed that they did not go head-to-head, but avoided direct competition. Instead, they determined where BigBox was *not* operating, and redirected their businesses. Carolyn related her analysis of stores in the adjacent county.

From Eli's perspective, it just goes to show that for CI to be able to rescue you, you cannot wait too long. You must act sooner rather than later. You can never recover time you have lost.

LOOKING BACK ONE YEAR LATER

Eli spoke with Carolyn at length before we left to learn from what she had learned. He later told us he then went to the next county and started visiting stores of the sort Carolyn had described. The owner of one of them, Frank, had been in a situation like Eli's and was doing better now with BigBox open than before BigBox opened. Frank told Eli his strategy was to "hit 'em where they ain't." In other words, Frank offered products and particularly services that BigBox did not. Frank offered to "give you a hand." Eli accepted.

Eli then immediately set to work, making Loder's into a true rural store, and also a destination. He made it comfortable, offering local products, and organic/trendy brands and products not offered at BigBox. He kept some products that BigBox offered, but decided, wisely, to offer them in much smaller sizes. He trained the staff to "walk with and work with" all customers, and never "leave them stranded on aisle 174 like at BigBox."

Loder's quickly became a place people enjoyed going to, where you could find "interesting" products and great service. For example, the repairs that Loder's already offered were moved to the front of the store. So, while Loder's could not sell a national brand chain saw for less than BigBox did, it could offer repairs that BigBox did not, and later sell the now-satisfied customer a more exclusive replacement brand that required fewer service calls. A good experience engendered trust. Things quickly turned around and Loder's was re-established in its new identity well before BigBox opened.

By the end of a year, Eli told us that he was considering joining Frank in a business aimed at helping firms facing future BigBox competition. He would be turning over Loder's to his two children sooner that he or they expected.

10

What Does This All Mean to You?

Who cares?

The short answer is everyone who touches or is touched by CI.

What you have seen, the behind-the-scenes look at CI rescues, applies not only to large firms, but to small ones as well. In fact, it applies to the DIYer. Why? Because how you do your job is not merely a matter of how good a researcher you are. If you cannot share what you know, the CI, with the right people, in the right way, and at the right time, you are not contributing to your firm's success. You are probably not contributing very much to your own.

UNDERSTANDING THE NATURE OF A CI RESCUE

There are some critical lessons that should emerge from our case studies because they are present there and in the business world:

- The end game is to have a CI process, with properly trained individuals (a part of the rescue process is to make sure there is ongoing training), which provides the end users with actionable intelligence. The CI must be produced, and then distributed, and then used. A failure at any point produces a total failure; a weakness at any point weakens the entire CI process.
- When hear of or read something that "works" elsewhere, think in terms of "adapt not just adopt." Your goal is not to replicate what some other firm does with respect to CI, but to replicate its success. It is successful, is not it? If not, why even study it?
- To be effective, CI must be a part of the firm or the organization, and not just bolted on. Think organic. Deal with things as they are.
- You cannot fix everything. You do not have the time, you probably do not have the authority, you—or your firm—probably do not have the money, and you certainly do not have the authority to effect that much change. Identify what

is most important. Then do what you can with that, and try and plant the seeds for continuing growth and change.
- Conduct your interviews, even of yourself, with extreme caution and care.
  - Never assume that what you are told, or what you believe, is correct. As our case studies show, people do not fully understand their own problems, and in some cases, even that they have problems. Always dig deeper; look, do not just listen—verify.
  - If you, your client, or your employer is a family or small firm, the dynamics can be very complex. First identify what is going on, with whom, and why. Then, and only then, start planning for possible change. You will often have to defer to the wishes, and prejudices, of key players. Work around—do not compete or confront.
- Since the goal of a CI rescue is producing and using actionable intelligence, studying what the end users receive and use is vital. You cannot look at just one piece of the process and expect to see it all. In particular, that means closely reviewing who uses what intelligence and how.
- Propose changes that make sense, not ones that look good to others.
- When the landscape is changing, it is hard to wait. But that is what you may have to do. If the CI rescue cannot wait, built meeting that change into your rescue. Be warned—even building in change does not always keep future, unforeseen, events from impacting the CI rescue.
- The CI rescue process involves a process of educating you and others. That education is a key to offering improvements and effecting substantive, permanent change.
- When you are faced with existing forces—documents, policies, procedures, and relationships—start by looking for ways to modify them rather than planning to replace them. Most people in business are more comfortable with what seems to be gradual change than what appears to be radical change. That is true even when the "gradual" change is actually quite radical. People are more comfortable accepting "improvements" to what they have built or are used to than they are with facing a "clean sweep."
- By offering "adjustments" to many elements, it becomes easier to suggest one or two more radical changes, such as eliminating one or two marginal intelligence "products."

USING THE DIAGNOSTICS QUIZZES MORE EFFECTIVELY

Throughout this book, you have seen the diagnostic quizzes used to dig into what is going on with each case. Here are some tips for using them more effectively in your CI rescue:

- A "yes" is not always a yes. Get the details supporting that "yes."
- A "possible," "maybe," or other intermediate answer can often point to a highly significant, but partially hidden, weakness. Try and disclose it before the harm can happen.

- A "no" answer almost always leads to another "no." The quiz comments are interconnected, so it is rare to get only one "no" and a lot of "yes."
- When interviewing, use open-end questions, and careful pauses, to bring out deeper responses from people to whom you speak. Remember our elicitation tips.
- The quizzes are not all-encompassing. Feel free to add to them. For example, they do not cover defending against the CI activities of competitors. There are several reasons for that:
  - Most CI processes that have been studied do not get involved in this.
  - Those CI teams that do this often prefer not to talk about what they do.
  - At some firms, this effort is the job of corporate security, or it a task spread among some combination of security, IT, legal, and intelligence.
  - Where it is done, it is often not done well because showing bottom line impact is difficult.
- After a CI rescue, use the quizzes to test what has been accomplished and to see what your CI rescue has accomplished—where is it actually working.

ABOUT CI RESEARCH AND ANALYSIS

There is, of course, more that everyone creating actionable CI, from the DIYers to the global team, can do better, but that is skill development, not process—and product—improvement. If you are doing CI, are thinking about doing it, or are trying to help others with CI, recognize the roles that research and analysis play in CI, and how to develop these skills. Let us discuss that for a moment:

- Merely learning about CI "on the fly" or "as we go" is almost never sufficient. In fact, it is rarely even marginally satisfactory. That does not have to happen, since there are many good sources for improving your research skills and honing your analytical talents.
- Education with respect to research and analysis should never stop. But the requirements for such continuing education differ with these two steps.
  - Education on research, both sources and techniques, should be ongoing. There are great books, blogs, training courses, webinars, and sessions at annual meetings of all sorts of organizations that can help. If you cannot find them, you are not looking. Education on research should be ongoing. No one can stop doing this—no one no matter how skilled or experienced.
  - Education on analysis is different. That is because intelligence analysis is not so much a skill that can be acquired, but a talent that can be nurtured and honed. Education on analysis should also never stop, but it is significantly different from education on research. Yes, you should look to the same sources as are available for education on research, but you must go further, deeper, and wider. To properly nurture and hone such analytical skills as you possess, you must continually expose yourself to a variety of intellectual challenges and eye-opening data. Try reading different books and magazines from what

you do now; then change that next year and the year after: move from history to news to archeology to science fiction to psychology, etc.

- Organization of the CI process can enable CI research and analysis to be effective and actionable—it cannot replace them.

Index

About the Authors

Carolyn M. Vella is the Founding Partner of The Helicon Group, a global competitive intelligence research, analysis, and consulting firm. In 2003, she was the recipient of the Society of Competitive Intelligence Professionals' Meritorious Award, the highest award SCIP can bestow. Vella has written numerous articles on business and competitive intelligence topics for publications including *Senior Exchange* and *Mergers & Acquisitions* and has been interviewed by *Business Digest*. She is the coauthor of eight books on competitive intelligence, including Praeger's *Bottom Line Competitive Intelligence, Improved Business Planning Using Competitive Intelligence*, and *The Internet Age of Competitive Intelligence*.

John J. McGonagle is the Managing Partner of The Helicon Group. He is the coauthor of eight books on competitive intelligence, including Praeger's *A Manager's Guide to Competitive Intelligence* and *Protecting Your Company Against Competitive Intelligence*. He also served as the research editor of the *Arthur Andersen European Community Sourcebook*. McGonagle received the prestigious Fellows Award in 1998 from SCIP, and in 2007, he received its highest award, the Meritorious Award. He has been an adjunct professor at Kutztown University and an adjunct lecturer at Lehigh University and Allentown College, teaching competitive intelligence (a course he developed) and business policy. McGonagle has served as a member and chair of the Association for Strategic Planning's Goodman Awards Committee for innovation in strategic planning.